Measuring the ERGs and BRGs

Ensuring Employee Resource Group Initiatives Drive Business and Organizational Results

Copyright © 2014 By Edward E. Hubbard, Ph.D. and Myra K. Hubbard, ABD

All rights reserved. The reproduction or utilization of this work in any form or by any electronic, mechanical or other means, known now or hereafter invented, including xerography, photocopying and recording and in any information storage and retrieval system, is forbidden without the written permission of Hubbard & Hubbard, Inc. This manual may not be changed or reprinted in any other form without written permission of the publisher. Printed in the United States of America.

ISBN 978-1-883733-16-2

Global Insights Publishing
832 Garfield Drive
Petaluma, CA 94954
Office: (707)763-8380   Fax:(435)674-1203

From the Author of the Best Selling Books: 'Measuring Diversity Results, The Diversity Scorecard, How to Calculate Diversity Return on Investment (DROI), and Diversity Training ROI

Acknowledgements

My first and deepest appreciation goes to my beautiful, caring wife, Myra. You are truly my soul-mate. God Blessed me tremendously with a wonderful gift in you. You constantly give me inspiration to continue to do this work. It was wonderful to collaborate with you in this project. I am so proud of you and the work you are doing in this field.

Secondly, I would like to thank my wonderful family. First, to my mother, Geneva Hubbard (in memoriam) whose love and strong foundation-setting values always keeps me strong. To my sons, sisters and their families as well as a host of other relatives who always keep us in their prayers. To Sheila and Phillip Parks, Berto, Pastor Shane and Tammy Wallis, and our church families at New Beginnings Christian Fellowship, New Life Christian Fellowship, The Springs SMCC Church. As well as many others too numerous to list…Thank You.

Ed

First and foremost, I would like to gratefully acknowledge and thank my awesome and brilliant husband, Ed. We have lived and worked together for many, many years and I appreciate and admire you more and more with each passing year. I know firsthand, no one walks on this journey of life alone. Ed, where do I start to thank you? You are my partner in life who supports me, believes in me, and urges me along the way to continuously build on my intuitive nature and insights. It was truly a pleasure to share the experience of writing this book with you.

I also, would like to thank our son, Chance. He takes time to faithfully check on his mom and dad to make sure we are "okay" and not working too hard. He often tells us he is proud of us and he values our advice and counsel. Thank you, we are proud of you too. And finally, we could not meet the demands of our travel schedules or perform the work we do without the constant support of our friends and extended family members---as I mentioned no one walks on this journey of life alone. Thanks to you all.

Myra

October, 2013

Table of Contents

Contents

Acknowledgements 3
Table of Contents 4
Preface 12
Who Should Read this Book 14
Chapter One: What are ERGs and BRGs? 15
    ERGs and BRGs Defined 15
    Types of Resource Groups 17
    Types of Employee Resource Groups in Organizations 18
    Functions and Practices of ERGs/BRGs 19
The Need to Demonstrate Business Impact 19
    ERG and BRG Measures of Success 20
    Importance of ERGs and BRGs 22
    References 23
Chapter Two: Aligning ERGs and BRGs with Organizational Strategy 24
    Aligning Across the Enterprise 24
    What is Top Management Support? 26
How Do You Begin the Formal Alignment Process? 28
    Step 1: Start Thinking of Diversity and Inclusion Metrics as a Critical Part of the Business. 29
    Step 2: Learn the Business! 29

Step 3: Develop Measurement Strategies and Activities that Line Managers Want... 30

Step 4: Involve Top Management 31

Step 5: Develop Interventions that are Practical, How-To Approaches 31

Step 6: Get a Handle on Diversity R.O.I. (DROI®) 34

Step 7: Make Some "Hard-Nose" Decisions About What is Needed 39

How Are Diversity Training Analysis and Evaluation Linked to Diversity Measurement Alignment?... 41

Step 8: Get Away From a Program Orientation........................... 42

Step 9: Stick With It! 43

References.. 44

Chapter Three: The Hubbard ERG BRG ROI Analysis Model 46

Introduction... 46

DROI®: A Systematic Approach to Measurement 46

Business Needs Analysis 49

Data Collection 51

Hubbard Diversity 9-S Framework 53

Shared Vision.. 53

Shared Values 54

Standards... 55

Strategy 56

Structure 57

Systems 58

Skills 59

Style 60

Staff	61
Creating an Integrated Picture of the Diversity Effort	62
Data Analysis	66
Isolating Diversity's Contribution	67
Convert the Contribution to Money	67
Calculating the ERG/BRG Initiative Costs	68
Calculating the DROI®	68
Identifying Intangible Benefits	68
Reporting & Tracking Progress	69
Communicating Results	69
Tracking and Assessing Progress	69
The Role of ERGs and BRGs in Creating ROI	69
Identifying ERG and BRG Deliverables	70
Developing a High-Performance Work Environment	72
Alignment with Strategy	73
Diversity Efficiency: Core versus Strategic Measures	74
Final Thoughts	77
References	77
Further Reading	78
Chapter Four: Prepare and Collect Data	79
Introduction	79
Identify Data Collection Measurement Areas	79
Figuring Out What to Measure that is Value-Added	80
Definitions:	80
Examples of Value-added Results	83
Diversity Value-added Results Method	87

Example of diversity results which support organizational goals 89

Reviewing Historical Data 90

Using Current Measures 91

Convert Current Measures to Usable Ones 92

Develop A Data Collection Plan for Performance Data 93

Developing New Measures 93

Typical Questions When Creating New Measures 94

Chapter Five: Isolate the ERG BRG Initiative Contribution 96

Introduction 96

A Common ERG/BRG Embarrassment 96

Diversity and the Double Standard Subterfuge 97

Preliminary Considerations 99

Diversity Value Chain Impact 99

Identifying Other Factors: A First Step 103

Participant Estimates of the ERG/BRG Initiative's Impact 106

Example of a Participant's Estimation 107

Typical Questions to Answer 108

Diversity Impact Questions 111

Supervisor Estimates of an ERG/BRG Initiative's Impact 116

Typical Questions to Ask Supervisors 116

Management Estimate of an ERG/BRG Initiative's Impact 120

Considerations When Selecting Isolation Strategies 121

Many ERG/BRG DROI Initiatives Will Generate Large Returns 122

Chapter Six: Convert the Contribution to Money 124

Introduction 124

Identifying the Hard and Soft Data Contained in the Diversity Contribution 124
Basic Steps to Convert Data 128
Strategies for Converting Data to Monetary Values 131
   Focus on a Unit of Improvement 132
   Determine a Value of Each Unit 132
   Calculate the Change in Performance Data 132
   Determine an Annual Amount for the Change 132
   Calculate the Annual Value of the Improvement 132
Converting the Contribution to Money 133
Strategy: Converting Output Data to Contribution 136
Strategy: Calculating the Cost of Quality 139
Strategy: Converting Employee Time 140
Strategy: Using Historical Costs 142
Strategy: Using Internal and External Experts' Input 143
Selecting the Appropriate Strategy 145
Accuracy and Credibility of the Data 147
   The Credibility Problem 147
How the Credibility of Data is Influenced 148
   Influence Factors 149
Making Adjustments 153

Chapter Seven: Calculating the Effectiveness and ROI Value Impact of ERGs and BRGs Initiatives 155
Introduction 155
Strategies for Accumulating and Calculating Costs 156
   Importance of Costs 156

The Impact of Reporting Costs without Benefits...................... 157
Typical Cost Categories... 158
  Diversity Initiative Cost Categories 159
Prorated vs. Direct Costs... 159
Benefits Factor 161
Needs Assessment... 161
Design and Development Costs 162
Acquisition Costs 163
Delivery Costs... 163
Evaluation 165
Overhead 166
Defining Return on Investment... 167
Summary: Calculating the Costs, Benefits, and Diversity ROI
Fundamentals... 171
Calculating the ERG/BRG Initiative Costs................................. 171
Calculating the DROI% 172
Identifying Intangible Benefits 173
Cautions When Using DROI 174
ERGs/BRGs are a Critical Link for Success................................ 178
Chapter Eight: Communicating Your ERG and BRG Success 179
Introduction... 179
General Reporting Principles.. 180
Key Questions to Answer when Selecting the Message 183
Developing the Evaluation Report.. 184
Management Summary 185
Background Information... 186

Evaluation Strategy 186

Data Collection, Analysis and Performance Tracking 187

ERG/BRG Initiative Costs and Benefits 188

Initiative Results and DROI® Calculations 188

Conclusions and Recommendations 189

Communicating Results to a Variety of Audiences 190

Other Means to Communicate Diversity Results 191

Reporting Your Results Should Not Be an Afterthought 192

Chapter Nine: Tracking and Assessing Progress 193

Introduction 193

What Does a Good Tracking System Look Like? 193

Monitoring Your DROI® Initiative's Progress 195

MetricLINK® an Automated Diversity Measurement System for Tracking Improved Performance 196

Other Measurement Software Options 199

Institutionalizing Your ERG/BRG Measurement System 200

Importance of Institutionalizing ERG/BRG Measurement and Tracking 202

Chapter Ten: Building an ERG BRG ROI Implementation Plan 203

Applying a Framework for Implementing Strategic Initiatives . 204

Analyzing Readiness for Change 209

C = P(SV)D > R 210

C = G(P) 225

Final Thoughts 228

About the Authors 232

Dr. Edward E. Hubbard Short Bio 232

Myra K. Hubbard Short Bio 233

Index 236

Hubbard & Hubbard, Inc. Products and Services.................….…..239
Metriclink Dashboard and Scorecard Services.................. 2

Comprehensive Online Performance Measurement and Management Services for Organizational Excellence......................... .2

Performance Spotlights and Publishing Opportunities 3

Preface

There has been an evolution and growth of employee resource groups (ERGs) over the last 30 years. First, the name has changed. Once called affinity groups, they are referred to not only as employee resource groups, but other names as well. They are also referred to as associate-resource groups, business network groups, employee networks and most recently, employee business resource groups (BRGs). Some groups started out as purely "interest groups". Their purpose was to provide employees who share common interests, lifestyles and beliefs with the opportunity to meet, network and provide encouragement and support for each other. These support groups were somewhat informal by nature, loosely defined and were based specifically on common needs and interests of participating employees.

Some general common practices of ERGs include: providing cultural support and diversity insight in company products, missions, or methods; developing products and branding for diverse target markets; and building company reputation through active community involvement. In addition, ERGs often provide resources for professional development, fostering a learning environment for better company contributions. Some ERGs are active in employee recruitment and engagement, attracting employees who identify with the company from the very start. Talent acquisition, communication with executives, culture awareness and change, and development are often at the core of ERG functioning. Employee Resource Groups and Business Resource Groups have become increasingly important to organizations that want to demonstrate a high level of success in their diversity and inclusion efforts.

They discovered that one way internal resources can contribute to a company's business objectives is to use them as an Employee Resource Group (ERG) or convert them to Business Resource Groups. These groups have a primary focus to assist the organization in meeting its strategic business goals and objectives. There is growing pressure on both Employee Resource Groups and Business Resource Groups to show measureable results for their initiatives, programs, and company-sponsored events. As companies continue to look for ways to cut costs and improve financial returns there is increasing interest in establishing Business Resource Groups and transforming ERGs to BRGs that have the skills to measure the ROI of their initiatives. This book provides a comprehensive, yet practical approach for aligning, collecting, analyzing and reporting the ROI impact of all ERG and BRG initiatives.

Chapter 1, *"What are ERGs and BRGs"* provides a definition of Employee Resource Groups and Business Resource Groups as well as an overview of their history and evolution in a business context. **Chapter 2**, *"Aligning ERGs and BRGs with Organizational Strategy"* explains the importance of strategically aligning ERG/BRG initiatives with the organization's strategic goals and objectives. **Chapter 3**, *"The Hubbard ERG BRG ROI Analysis Model"* outlines four time-tested ROI-focused analysis phases that produces a comprehensive and systematic framework for analyzing the ROI impact of ERG/BRG initiatives. These steps are designed for today's fast-paced, need –it-yesterday business environment. They save ERG/BRG members time, enhance their productivity with each step and improve their ability to produce high quality performance improvement interventions that drive business goals, objectives and ROI. **Chapter 4**, *"Prepare and Collect Data"* meticulously guides you through critical data collection requirements to produce value-added results. **Chapter 5**, *"Isolate the ERG BRG Initiative Contribution"* will help you select a method to isolate your ERG/BRG initiative's contribution to the organization's goals and objectives versus other contributing factors. **Chapter 6**, *"Convert the Contribution to Money"* walks you through specific strategies to convert either hard or soft data to monetary values. **Chapter 7**, *"Calculating the Effectiveness and ROI Value Impact of ERGs and BRGs Initiatives"* contains a detailed process to calculate the ROI value of ERG and BRG initiatives. It is complete with formulas and examples to illustrate their application to show evidence-based results of the ERG/BRG initiative's impact. **Chapter 8**, *"Communicating Your ERG and BRG Success"* explains a few general principles that are important when communicating your ERG/BRG initiative's results. **Chapter 9**, *"Tracking and Assessing Progress"* explains some key considerations for tracking and assessing the overall progress of your ERG/BRG ROI initiatives. **Chapter 10**, "Building an ERG BRG ROI Implementation Plan" completes the book with a discussion of the essential ingredients needed to successfully implement your ERG/BRG initiatives and methods to manage the elements of change that are generated when these actions are set in motion.

Who Should Read this Book

This book is designed specifically for Employee Resources Group and Business Resource Group Leaders, Members and their Sponsors. It is also useful for Chief Diversity Officers, Diversity Directors, Diversity Managers, ERG and BRG allies, and any others who have responsibilities for and/or interest in the successful operation of an ERG and/or BRG. It will help ERGs and BRGs save time, resources and efforts when developing methods to measure and demonstrate the financial ROI impact their initiatives are having on the organization's bottom-line. It is a "must read" for any group that wants to highlight their success in performance improvement terms and impact!

Chapter One: What are ERGs and BRGs?

ERGs and BRGs Defined

As organizations leverage the presence of diversity in the workforce, we have seen an increase in the existence of employee resource groups and business resource groups. There has been an evolution and growth of employee resource groups over the last 30 years. First, the name has changed. Once called affinity groups, they are referred to not only as employee resource groups, but other names as well. They are also referred to as associate-resource groups, business network groups, employee networks and most recently, employee business resource groups. Some groups started out as purely "interest groups". Their purpose was to provide employees who share common interests, lifestyles and beliefs with the opportunity to meet, network and provide encouragement and support for each other. These support groups were somewhat informal by nature, loosely defined and were based specifically on common needs and interests of participating employees.

An organization's continued success requires that we maintain a work environment where all employees feel valued, respected and able to contribute to their fullest potential, regardless of similarities and differences. Diversity BRGs further this goal by:

- Serving as employee support and providing networking opportunities for members;

- Sponsoring relevant programs for professional and personal growth;
- Sponsoring or participating in education/awareness activities and events;
- Sharing with the Diversity Council perceived obstacles/barriers to success or satisfaction;
- Acting as liaison, or participating in community outreach and volunteer programs;
- Supporting employee recruitment and retention initiatives;
- Supporting marketing efforts in targeted communities.

Though the terms are often used interchangeably, there appears to be a major distinction being highlighted when forming an ERG or BRG. The name change signifies a movement away from their goals of supporting diversity and inclusion to being broader and more business focused. As the name changes, the number of ERGs are increasing. The 2011 report by Mercer and a study by Catalyst in 2009 noted that even when the economy was slowing down, the development of ERGs was on the rise.

Employee Resource Groups (ERGs) are independent, voluntary groups of employees who share common interest. Business Resource Groups are similar to Employee Resource Groups but are also aligned with the company's business objectives. Given the latest evolution of the transformation from ERGs to business resource groups (BRGs), The Center for Effective Organizations (CEO) hypothesizes that the movement to BRGs is a function of the current need for organizations to innovate. CEO concludes, as ERGs become more linked to the needs of the organization, their funding will grow, their influence will expand, their impact will increase, and the evolution will continue.

Historically, companies have started with resource groups for Blacks and women, and in their early versions, many of these were more social in nature. Employee Resource Groups (ERGs) began as race-based employee forums that were created in response to racial tension in the 1960s. ERGs got their start in 1964 when Joseph Wilson, the CEO of the Xerox Corporation along with the organization's African American employees formed the first caucus group in order to address the issue of discrimination and to help create a fair corporate environment. As president of Xerox, he made an effort to integrate Xerox during the late 1960s. After the race riots that began in Detroit had reached Xerox headquarters in Rochester, New York, Wilson wrote in a letter to all Xerox managers that "he wanted a very aggressive program to recruit and hire blacks in this company". Xerox launched the National Black Employees Caucus in 1970 and later followed with the formation of the Black Women's Leadership Caucus (BWLC). Early in their history, these groups also called affinity groups were a tactic of advocating for equal pay and equal opportunity.

Types of Resource Groups

There are numerous types of ERGs existing at different companies. While the number of companies responding was not reported, the following list represents the top employee resource groups (ERGs), as determined by Diversity Best Practices 2011 benchmarking and assessment:

Types of Employee Resource Groups in Organizations

	Types of Employee Resource Groups	
	Women	89%
	Lesbian, Gay, Bisexual & Transgender Employees	73%
	Multicultural Women and Men	62%
	Military Veterans	46%
	People with Disabilities	46%
	Generational groups	42%
	Working parents	31%
	Religious groups	23%
	Single parents	8%

With women accounting for more than half of the country's working population, women's employee resource groups are the most common within companies. Eighty-nine percent of companies responding to Diversity Best Practices benchmarking survey report having an ERG for women. While people must self-identify to be recognized as a lesbian, gay, bisexual or transgender employee, 73 percent of Diversity Best Practices benchmarking and assessment participants offer a resource group for these workers. Nearly two-thirds (62 percent) of all Diversity

Best Practices benchmarking and assessment companies offer employee resources groups for multicultural women and men.

Employee resource groups for military veterans have been gaining popularity in recent years. Forty-six percent of responding companies offer an affinity group for these employees. Nearly half (46 percent) of all companies participating in Diversity Best Practices' benchmarking and assessment offer an employee resource group for people with disabilities. Diversity Best Practices (n.d.).

Functions and Practices of ERGs/BRGs

Some general common practices of ERGs include: providing cultural support and diversity insight in company products, missions, or methods; developing products and branding for diverse target markets; and building company reputation through active community involvement. In addition, ERGs often provide resources for professional development, fostering a learning environment for better company contributions. Some ERGs are active in employee recruitment and engagement, attracting employees who identify with the company from the very start. Talent acquisition, communication with executives, culture awareness and change, and development are often at the core of ERG functioning.

The Need to Demonstrate Business Impact

Making the business case requires ERGs and BRGs to diagnose the effectiveness of their work and learn to calculate return on investment for their efforts. The Center for Effective Organizations suggests that the groups need to be provided with skills to understand data well enough to diagnose the impact of their work. Using data to discover new opportunities and problems to be solved requires developing diagnostic analytical skills. Driving measurable business requires measurement of results and communicating those linkages between action taken and results. Welbourne, T.M., & McLaughlin, L.L. (2013, June). *Making the business case for employee resource groups.* Paper presented at the Employee Resource Group Leadership Summit, El Segundo, CA.

Evaluation is normally conducted to determine if initiative or program objectives are achieved or if the achievement of the objectives results in enhanced performance of the individual on the job (Collins, 2001). The evaluation of HRD programs is focused not only on individual success and individual performance on the job, but on actual outcomes including financial impact or return on investment (ROI) (Van Buren, 2001). Evaluation is a systematic process by which data are collected and converted into information for measuring the effects of the initiative, helping in decision making, documenting results to be used in organizational improvement, and providing a method for determining the quality of the initiative (Basarab & Root, 1992). Due to the increasing need to develop and implement results-based ERG initiatives, organizations are looking for a more systematic approach to evaluation.

ERG and BRG Measures of Success

Employee Resource Groups and Business Resource Groups have become increasingly important to organizations that want to demonstrate a high level of success in their diversity and inclusion efforts (Ross,

2011). They discovered that one way internal resources can contribute to a company's business objectives is to use them as an Employee Resource Group (ERG) or Business Resource Group. These groups, which are sometimes referred to as Business Resource Groups (BRGs). There is growing pressure on Employee Resource Groups to show measureable results of their diversity initiatives, programs, and company-sponsored events. As companies continue to look for ways to cut costs and improve financial returns there is increasing interest in establishing Business Resource Groups and transforming ERGs to BRGs.

A successful ERG or BRG is one that is aligned to the priorities of the company, can measure its progress and can show a return on investment (Deloitte, 2010). Deloitte Consulting LLP points out there are several challenges facing ERGs and BRGs demonstrating value to the organization such as: (1) some resource groups believe their activities are not measurable, (2) it is difficult for ERGs or BRGs to prove cause and effect, (3) ERGs and BRGs are unsure which metrics and indicators are important to the company, (4) ERGs and BRGs do not consistently track their progress towards metrics and indicators, and (5) Employee Resource Groups do not communicate outcomes consistently.

There is a lack of detailed studies and ERG/BRG books on the market that provide an analysis methodology which views the work of the ERG and/or BRG in a holistic manner or provide a definitive process illustrating how Employee Resource Groups and Business Resource Groups drive key performance indicators.

Importance of ERGs and BRGs

One of the primary trends in workplace diversity and inclusion in organizations is the establishment and utilization of Employee Resource Groups and Business Resource Groups. The interest in accountability and ERG's/BRG's impact on business outcomes has been driven by a number of factors including (1) increased costs of supporting the groups, (2) reduced budgets within organizations, (3) lack of measurement, (4) unclear outcomes from the groups, (5) competition for funding, (6) competing time commitments, and (7) senior management interest in the group's performance and return-on-investment for use of company dollars.

The Industrial Relations Counselors, Inc. sponsored Mercer, a consulting, outsourcing and investment services organization to conduct a study of Employee Resource Groups. This research highlights a need to have Employee Resource Groups align their work with the business (Mercer, 2011). What was not addressed in the Mercer study was "how" the groups can systematically and consistently align their initiatives with the business needs. The available literature contains articles with definitions of ERGs and BRGs, categories of ERGs, the benefits of ERGs and highlights of company business impact when utilizing their resource groups. What seemed to be missing from the literature was an informative, definitive process model or framework to guide their strategic business use. There was not a process to take an ERG or BRG beyond the initial stages of development and provide an approach for utilizing the group to drive key performance indicators and business outcomes. It is our intent to provide the missing elements along with ROI metrics and value proposition methodologies.

We hope this book will add to the literature by providing a guided, step-by-step, structured process to inform and educate ERGs/BRGs explaining how they can more consistently drive key performance indicators and business outcomes. In order to do this effectively, it will take a keen focus on alignment which we will explore in the next chapter.

References

Top Five Employee Resource Groups for U.S. Workers. Retrieved July 11, 2013, from http://www.diversitybestpractices.com/events/top-five-employee-resource-groups-us-workers?pnid=7739.

Chapter Two: Aligning ERGs and BRGs with Organizational Strategy

Aligning Across the Enterprise

Misaligned ERG/BRG metrics and initiatives, like cars out of alignment, can develop serious problems if they are not corrected quickly. Like the cars, they are hard to steer and don't respond well to changes in direction. Alignment is a response to the new business reality where organizational business requirements are in flux and competitive forces are turbulent, and the bonds of employee loyalty and engagement can be challenging. Old "representation-focused" approaches to diversity metrics are not strategic or performance-driven.

A familiar criticism of Diversity and Inclusion metrics, in general, is that they are oftentimes put together in a piecemeal fashion without a clear framework of how they are relevant to the current and future business needs of the organization. Many ERG/BRG interventions have the best intentions however they sometimes lack this alignment and/or linkage to the overall strategic direction of the firm. A great majority of the measurement approaches tend to focus primarily on "activities" rather than "evidence-based outcomes and targeted results". They are usually not built on comprehensive business needs assessments that are targeted to solve real business challenges.

In this chapter, we will discuss nine steps you can use to improve the alignment of your ERG/BRG's initiative metrics. This methodology also covers a wide range of actions to build practical approaches to verify the strategic business needs of the organization.

When it comes to alignment, we have observed that *"focusing on tactics without a strategic framework is like learning to run faster in the wrong direction"*. You cannot make a strategic contribution without a tight alignment and linkage to the business objectives and success metrics. If you want to have your interventions resonate with the C-suite and line managers, they must be based on real bottom-line needs that drive organizational performance. Whether the ERG/BRG initiative is diversity training to teach cultural competency skills, selling products to emerging market clientele, innovating new products and services for a global market, delivering healthcare services, serving governmental constituents, meeting a wide range of student needs, etc., strategically aligned ERG/BRG measurement strategies have the best chance at success and sustainability.

Let's take a look at an example that helps to clarify this relationship. First, let's say that among the organization's strategic objectives, your group has located a series of crucial performance areas. One of these areas focuses on an objective of improved customer service. Based upon the importance of this area to the business, the ERG/BRG has created a corresponding strategic objective to analyze and improve service across all demographic market segments. And in alignment with the Diversity Strategic Plan, your ERG/BRG has decided to examine possible opportunities to use the ERG/BRG's member resources to identify an initiative that will improve service to the targeted customer market.

In the second step, you determine that for service to be improved in these targeted markets, the critical success factor areas must include "improved communication", "culturally appropriate interactions", quick access, increased satisfaction, and accurate information. Finally, these critical success factor areas lead your group to select ERG/BRG performance measures and indicators that support each critical success factor area such as the "percentage of multilingual service transactions delivered", "number of rings to answer", "percentage of favorable response on the diverse customer satisfaction survey", etc. This type of alignment drives improved performance and gains top management support.

What is Top Management Support?

Top management support is not a speech or a memo; it is real actions taken by the leadership function in an organization that under girds building a successful diverse and inclusive work environment. It is not something nice that the President or CEO of the organization mentions in a speech. It is a continuing commitment backed up by words and deeds over a sustained period of time. It means a strong personal involvement on the part of management in shaping the diversity vision and accountability of leaders, employees and others. In a word…it requires commitment.

Diversity leadership commitment can be defined as demonstrated evidence and actions taken by leaders to support, challenge and champion the diversity process within their organization. It reflects the degree to which the organization's leaders utilize behaviors that set the diversity vision, direction, and policy into actual practice. It also reflects the individual level and degrees of accountability leaders take in helping ERGs/BRGs forge a practical implementation strategy. Diversity leadership commitment as a practice is reflected in the level of specific behavior they exhibit as a model diversity champion. If your ERG/BRG is to garner this kind of support, your initiatives must resonate with the organization's business strategy in such a way that the C-Suite and your Sponsor/Champion can see the "line of sight" connection with the strategic goals and objectives of the organization.

From an organizational change point of view, Diversity leadership commitment is the behavior that helps establish a direction or goal for change (a vision), provides a sense of urgency and importance for the vision, facilitates the motivation of others, and cultivates necessary conditions for achievement of the vision. Diversity leadership commitment is critical to the organization change process. It cannot be delegated or given just tacit consideration. It is clear that the CEO of the organization and heads of the main operating units have primary responsibility for breakthrough progress on diversity. If they do not hold themselves accountable for the leadership requirements to execute diversity initiatives (such as ERG/BRG initiatives), the change effort is doomed to failure. Diversity officers and their staffs have a crucial role to play as facilitators of the diversity change process. And, ERG/BRG members have a key role in building and maintaining its momentum. Leaders alone cannot be held responsible for making it happen. Your group must build skills and competence to develop the intellectual muscle to plan, direct, control, and support any strategic improvement effort. As a unifying force, Diversity commitment throughout the organization serves as a key lynchpin for success that when combined with strategic actions will sustain forward progress.

ERG/BRG performance processes that help sustain alignment can be broken down into three steps: the first step involves identifying specific value-added diversity objectives your ERG/BRG will work on; the second step involves determining where and how the organization must succeed to accomplish each ERG/BRG performance objective, spelling out the where's and how's as a set of *critical success factor areas*; and finally, selecting ERG/BRG performance measures for each critical success factor area. These measures help determine if the organization is in fact performing well on its objectives. ERG/BRG performance measures are the tools your group will use to determine whether you are meeting your objectives and moving toward the successful implementation of your ERG/BRG strategy.

How Do You Begin the Formal Alignment Process?

If you want to successfully align your ERG/BRG initiatives with the business strategy of the organization, you can utilize a 9-Step Method to improve and effectively calibrate your work.

[handwritten annotations:
1. identify objectives
2. determine critical success factors
3. select performance measurements]

Step 1: Start Thinking of Diversity and Inclusion Metrics as a Critical Part of the Business.

It is important to discard the notion or idea that ERG/BRG initiatives are separate from the rest of the organization or can be addressed by simply implementing a series of well-intentioned activities. All ERG/BRG interventions must be measured and integrated with the on-going operational activities of the organization. It requires conducting an analysis to set as top priority those metrics that help the organization meet its strategic objectives.

It is also important to get <u>copies of the organization's strategic business plans and mine them for ideas, impacts and consequences.</u> Meet with key managers to talk about their plans. Determine where they will need the ERG/BRG support your group can provide and identify a set of key ROI-based metrics to measure your success. You should also look for new technologies, organizational changes, new product lines and new company directions your ERG/BRG can support.

Step 2: Learn the Business!

Knowing the business is critical to the alignment process. If you want to talk with managers coherently about their challenges, you must know the business and how it affects their business, especially the financial end. It is crucial to know things such as "Company Earning per Share", "Net Profit as a Percent of Sales", "Gross Profit Margin", "Net Income", etc. It is important to talk with colleagues in the accounting and strategic planning departments about the state of the business. Study the annual reports and anything else your group can get its hands on until you are comfortable with the company's financial objectives and competitive position. Know the company's ROI numbers, sales figures, operating profit, debt-to-equity ratios and cash flows.

Your ERG/BRG should be conversant about new business ventures and the company's direction. Know your company's products and services. Learn what's selling, what's not and why. Alignment requires that you are able to identify with line management priorities to build understanding and credibility.

Step 3: Develop Measurement Strategies and Activities that Line Managers Want

Start identifying "business and line department priorities" first, and then focus on ERG/BRG priorities. This is called being "other-centered". It improves the ERG/BRG's measurement alignment by creating a business context for developing ROI-based solutions. Use your study of strategic plans, operating reports and talks with line managers to locate an appropriate set of metrics to evaluate your ERG/BRG's intervention impact. It is critical to get customer and Sponsor input and feedback on your proposed initiatives.

Step 4: Involve Top Management

Top management's involvement is critical in the alignment process. Therefore it is important to interview them and ask what organizational needs they consider important. You must complete research at all levels of the organization to create a comprehensive measurement strategy.

Develop a master plan by department, level and/or position to focus your ERG/BRG metrics strategy. This means conducting a utility analysis to determine which metrics are "critical", "Important", or "nice to include" to effectively assess the success of the ERG/BRG intervention. Use leaders and managers as much as possible as subject matter experts versus your own process knowledge to gauge what performance gaps that exist. Once the specific gaps are known, an appropriate ERG/BRG intervention can be designed.

Step 5: Develop Interventions that are Practical, How-To Approaches

Many organizations will say they have diversity measures in place. However, when you actually check them, you find that they are simply people and/or activity counts. They'll look around and say they've established a council or have had a particular celebration on a particular day. And while those are important, senior leaders don't always see these things as bottom-line outcomes. They're not looking at how the ERG/BRG initiative process has increased market penetration in key ethnic markets or how the ERG/BRG initiative process has added 'X' number of customers or how the ERG/BRG initiative process has helped remove obstacles and produced a cadre of "promotion-ready", high-potential employees who can now reach their full potential. Progressive ERGs/BRGs show how they have utilized ERG/BRG technologies to integrate ERG/BRG initiative processes into productivity improvement issues, product quality issues, innovation challenges and people performance issues.

To have credibility, ERG/BRG interventions must be developed in a way that seamlessly integrate with key organizational priorities at critical levels and are designed in a way that employees can use them right away to improve the organization's functioning. To accomplish this, it may require having the flexibility to move away from pure "academic images" of Diversity and Inclusion theory and venture into the realm of the "live-lab" of real organizational problems and challenges. It may involve enhancing the environment by working in the ERG/BRG, with a keen focus on "social networking and mentoring." It means working "hand-in-hand" with line managers as strategic business partners to solve some of the messy problems of performance improvement and change. These challenges and the need for change must be verified with an effective Business Needs Analysis in order to show the benefits and ROI impact. Part of your role as members of the ERG/BRG, is to ask yourself...who am I developing this intervention for...to go along with the latest fad that other organization's are using or helping my organization address internal (or external) challenges to help solve real business challenges?

This doesn't mean ERGs/BRGs cannot have a purpose to develop its members or provide an improved climate for social networking and inclusion as a primary goal. It merely suggests that a key strategy for sustainability for both the ERG/BRG and the organization is to meet the strategic challenges of the organization head on.

It is important to stay clear of theories and fads that are not strategically tied to producing organization-enhancing results. Sure, some of them can help create "out-of-the-box" thinking that may help produce new, practical approaches that could generate value. However, these ideas need to be well researched and tested for their practical strategic value and potential impact before they become the centerpiece of the group's work.

It is also critical to limit "Diversity and Inclusion speak" when working with internal clients and sponsors. Your audience does not have to be masters of it. It may take a while to gain credibility from their vantage point. This credibility will come faster when you are able to demonstrate specific, measurable results in quantitative and qualitative terms as a result of the work you have completed together. The results and outcomes of the ERG/BRG initiatives must show how the results are tied to the organization's bottom-line impact. The results you obtain will improve your level of credibility, commitment and involvement, not the merits of theories and fads alone.

Step 6: Get a Handle on Diversity R.O.I. (DROI®)

DROI® is a registered trademark of Hubbard & Hubbard, Inc. All rights reserved.

It is absolutely essential to master the technologies of Diversity ROI (DROI®) analytics and measurement processes for all of the interventions your ERG/BRG provides. It is critical to identify interventions, programs, and activities that have a measurable impact on organizational and employee performance.

We have always thought of ERGs/BRGs as professional groups chartered to improve the organizational experience. However, if they are to be taken seriously as a strategic partner, they must possess a structure, framework and critical components that are consistent with other serious partner relationships. For example, if we examine the strategic partners who work in Marketing, Sales Operations, and the like, we would find they all have well-defined competencies, proven theories, and applied sciences that under gird their application. These theories and sciences provide a recognized structure, strategy and a set of measurable standards to guide those who work in the field.

If we examine the disciplines that include doctors, engineers, lawyers, and others, they must be certified to practice their craft. There are also certifications for human resource professionals such as the PHR, SPHR, and GPHR certifications offered by the Society for Human Resource Management (SHRM) for Human Resource Professionals, the HPI certification for Trainers by the American Society for Training and Development (ASTD), or the CPT certification for Organization Development professionals offered by the International Society for Performance Improvement (ISPI).

The Hubbard Diversity Measurement and Productivity (HDM&P) Institute and the Hubbard Diversity ROI Institute offers six diversity certifications based on its Diversity ROI® and Diversity ROI Analytics® methodology such that ERG/BRG group members can utilize strategic Diversity measurement and ROI sciences to implement their initiatives:

- Certified Diversity Trainer® (CDT)
- Certified Diversity Advisor® (CDA)
- Certified Diversity Performance Consultant® (CDPC)
- Certified Diversity Business Partner® (CDBP)
- Certified Diversity Strategist® (CDS)
- Certified Diversity Intervention Specialist® (CDIS)

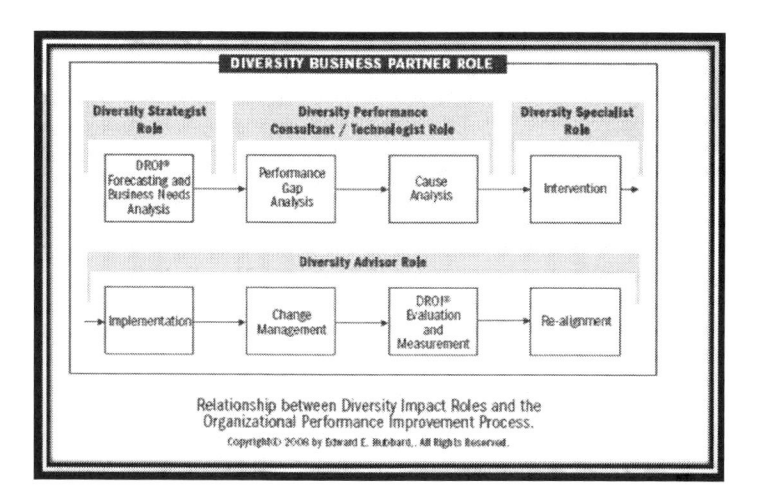

Relationship between Diversity Impact Roles and the Organizational Performance Improvement Process.
Copyright© 2008 by Edward E. Hubbard. All Rights Reserved.

These fields of study contain specific, identifiable roles that are performed, areas of expertise that allow an ERG/BRG member to build specialized concentrations of skills and knowledge within the discipline, detailed outputs produced by these roles, as well as a model of measurable competencies that define specific behaviors that enable the work to be completed with a high degree of accuracy and effectiveness. This training is available for ERG/BRG members at all levels and ERG/BRG members can be certified in any of the certification areas, especially the Certified Diversity Advisor® (CDA), Certified Diversity Performance Consultant® (CDPC), and Certified Diversity Intervention Specialist® (CDIS) disciplines which are designed to support their initiatives and intervention work.

As a professional strategic partner, ERG/BRG practices must align with key objectives and outcomes to operate with similar standards built on a solid framework of both concept and science.

These practices must be delivered through the work of competent, credible ERG/BRG members using clear standards of excellence linked to business performance. Using your talents and skills, based upon a competency-rich Diversity Discipline Framework™, ERGs? BRGs will be able to integrate the ideas underlying Diversity and Inclusion with specific measurement strategies and organizational systems theory to create a talent-enriched, innovative climate that utilizes its diverse resources more effectively. Getting a handle on ROI means identifying units of measure for the interventions and activities that have a measurable impact on performance. ERGs/BRGs must consistently apply measurement sciences, track their interventions, and publish them as Diversity ROI studies such that they can be utilized as "best practices".

Sample measures which support an ERG/BRG Diversity ROI measurement alignment strategy include covering key Diversity Scorecard perspectives such as:

Workforce Profile Perspective
- Diversity Hit Rate
- #/ % Minorities as Officials and Managers
- #/% Diversity Survival and Loss Rate
- #/% Turnover by Length of Service

Workplace Climate and Culture Profile Perspective
- % Favorable Ratings on Cultural Audit Demographic Group
- "Employer of Choice" Ratings versus Top 5-10 Competitors
- Retention Rates of Critical Human Capital
- # and Type of Policies and Procedures Assessed for Diverse Workforce Impact

It is important to design evaluations and utilize metrics that are practical and reflect a systemic analysis. For example, use before and after measures which examine your ERG/BRG intervention results compared to key measures which are already established and utilized in the organization.

It is also imperative that you are cautious and careful with the procedure to demonstrate how you isolated the Diversity ROI value from all other possible interventions (that could have contributed to the organizational benefit). Be careful what you take credit for. In a Diversity ROI study, it is important that you only list those outcomes you can control which demonstrate a "chain-of-impact" to the outcome. ERG/BRG intervention outputs are "inputs" that fuel contributions to line results. There are usually many intervening variable in the outcome production process. Isolation techniques must include utilizing scientific processes such as control groups, time-series analysis, forecast estimates, participant estimates, etc., to attribute the ERG/BRG's intervention contribution to specific business outcomes and benefits (separate and apart from other contributors).

Step 7: Make Some "Hard-Nose" Decisions About What is Needed

It is essential to conduct a comprehensive Business Assessment or "Needs Analysis" to determine what interventions are necessary to meet the intent of the organization's business objectives. For example, when evaluating an organizational challenge, an ERG/BRG may be partial to a favorite diversity intervention or solution regardless of the problem or need. It is crucial that a scientific approach is taken where effective data collection helps determine the appropriate response, not what the ERG/BRG favors. Performing a comprehensive Needs Analysis is the cornerstone of implementing a solid, credible performance improvement process. It helps ERG/BRGs make "hard-nosed" decisions and provide an appropriate justification for either developing or not developing a specific intervention. ERGs/BRGs *must* conduct a needs analysis, no matter how abbreviated, before any intervention development takes place.

If a Diversity Training intervention is required, for example, the objectives of the Needs Analysis are to:
- Describe the *exact nature* of a performance discrepancy

- Determine the *cause(s)* of the discrepancy
- Recommend the appropriate *solution(s)*
- Describe the *learner population*

In general, Training Needs Analysis consists of the following steps.

- Step 1: Identify and describe the performance discrepancies.
- Step 2: Determine the causes of the discrepancies.
- Step 3: Identify those performance discrepancies that are based on lack of skill or knowledge. Then identify the skills and knowledge needed that is related to diversity and diversity competence.
- Step 4: Determine whether diversity training or another intervention is a viable solution.
- Step 5: Recommend solutions.
- Step 6: Describe the performer's and organization's role in behaviorally specific terms that relate to diversity excellence and performance.

How Are Diversity Training Analysis and Evaluation Linked to Diversity Measurement Alignment?

A Training Needs Analysis establishes the criteria for measuring the success of training after its completion. A thorough needs analysis should answer the question:

"What good *will* training do?"

A thorough Diversity ROI training evaluation will answer the question:

"What good *did* training do and what was the Return on Investment (DROI)?"

An effective Diversity ROI training evaluation **cannot** be conducted unless a thorough needs analysis has been completed. We cannot determine what was accomplished by a Diversity training intervention or program unless we have first defined what the program was **intended** to accomplish. The Diversity training needs analysis provides baseline measures against which to judge our Diversity training efforts and will help us make the hard-nosed decisions about what is the best way to meet our internal/external client's need.

Step 8: Get Away From a Program Orientation

Diversity is not a program; it is a process of systemic organizational change. Programs have a beginning and an end. However, people will never be finished with their differences. Therefore ERG/BRG interventions and the metrics that support them must reflect a range that supports the systems and processes that drive real organizational performance over the long-term. The context for ERG/BRG performance is the organization's business and its objectives. To be relevant and aligned, it is critical to think in terms of the business, its goals, objectives and its performance needs (interventions that drive financial metrics such as Dollar Share of Market, Revenue per Customer, Cost Reduction, etc.). It requires ERGs/BRGs to connect to and work in concert with all levels of the organization.

It is reported that many top and senior executives truly support their ERGs/BRGs, but feel they should play a stronger strategic role in the growth and development of the organization. They expect ERGs/BRGs to help increase productivity and provide solutions that generate a stronger competitive edge. In effect, both top and line managers are seeking ERGs/BRGs that function as "strategic business partners" to solve real business problems which have a bottom-line impact on the organization's day-to-day and strategic priorities. To successfully align and link ERG/BRG strategies with the organization's strategic business plan, you must actively pursue top and line managers regarding their specific business problems and speak their language. For example, if you are working with the Finance department, you must be able to talk about their problems and potential solutions in financial terms, impacts and consequences. If the problem is focused in the operations area, ERGs/BRGs must talk in operational terms, etc.

Step 9: Stick With It!

Developing a Diversity ROI measurement capability is a "skill". And like any skill ERGs/BRGs must learn what it is, understand its applications, use it, study the feedback from its use and refine the skill until the group builds a strategic level of competency. There is an expectation that the group will be able to demonstrate their initiatives produce "value-added" results for the organization and themselves. We expect doctors, engineers, social scientists, technicians, etc., to have mastered their craft in order to trust the solutions and alternatives they suggest. The same is true for ERG/BRG-focused efforts. You must hold the ERG/BRG members to a high standard whether or not your C-Suite executives and others ask for it. The Hubbard ERG and BRG ROI Institute specializes in a wide range of programs, tools, online learning, and certification training to help build highly credible skills in this vital business discipline.

A critical element of meeting that standard is an effective use of Diversity ROI skills that build a strategic alignment with the strategy, structure and systems that drive the organization's performance. It is imperative to take advantage of learning and listening opportunities that broaden our understanding, build Diversity ROI capability as well as business acumen.

It's not easy. It will take lots of work and a heavy persistence for excellence. It requires ERGs/BRGs to possess an internal standard that says we do not accept being mediocre in our work. Developing this expertise won't happen overnight or without setbacks and frustrations, but it can be done and is worth the struggle. This means that as ERG/BRG members, you must develop a "strategic alignment mindset" that places your Diversity ROI measurement efforts on par with any discipline that drives business results and success!

References

Hubbard, Edward E. *How to Calculate Diversity Return on Investment.* California: Global Insights Publishing, 1999.

Hubbard, Edward E. *The Diversity Scorecard: Evaluating the Impact of Diversity on Organizational Performance.* Massachusetts: Butterworth-Heinemann, Elsevier Publishing, 2004.

Hubbard, Edward E. *The Diversity Discipline: Implementing Diversity Work with a Strategy, Structure, and ROI Measurement Focus.* California: Global Insights Publishing, 2009.

Chapter Three: The Hubbard ERG BRG ROI Analysis Model

Introduction

Interest in diversity and the return-on-investment associated with it is increasing. Several issues such as changing national workforce demographics and the global economy are driving this increased interest and its application to a wide range of related issues. Pressures from senior managers, Boards of Directors, stockholders, and clients to show the return on diversity investment is probably the most influential driver. Competitive economic pressures are causing intense scrutiny of all expenditures, including all diversity costs such as ERG and BRG budgets. In addition, ERGs and BRGs know they must begin to show how what they do is linked to the bottom line in hard numbers. In short, they must calculate and report their diversity ROI like any other part of the business.

DROI®: A Systematic Approach to Measurement

Calculating Diversity Return on Investment (DROI®) requires asking key questions and performing key tasks along the way. To achieve a successful result, measuring the DROI® generated from

ERG/BRG initiatives requires a systematic approach that takes into account both costs and benefits. The Hubbard ERG/BRG ROI Model^{tm}, as shown in the figure below, provides a step-by-step approach that keeps the process manageable so ERG/BRG members can tackle one issue at a time.

The Hubbard ERG/BRG ROI Model^{tm} consists of *nine* time tested steps that produces a comprehensive and systematic framework for analyzing the ROI impact of ERG/BRG initiatives. These steps are designed for today's fast-paced, need –it-yesterday business environment. They save ERG/BRG members time, enhance their productivity with each step and improve their ability to produce high quality performance improvement interventions that drive business goals, objectives and ROI. The model also emphasizes that this logical, systematic process flows from one step to another. Applying the model provides consistency from one analysis phase and DROI® calculation to another. In essence, it suggests that the major aspects of measuring the ROI impact of your ERG and BRG initiatives include the following:

1. **Reviewing the Organization's Business Strategy**
2. **Identifying Diversity Objectives linked to Business Challenges**
3. **Identifying ERG/BRG Objectives Linked to Diversity Strategy**
4. **Collecting Data and Analyze It**

5. **Isolating Diversity's Contribution**
6. **Converting the Contribution to Money**
7. **Calculating Cost, Benefits, and DROI**
8. **Communicating Results**
9. **Tracking and Assessing Progress**

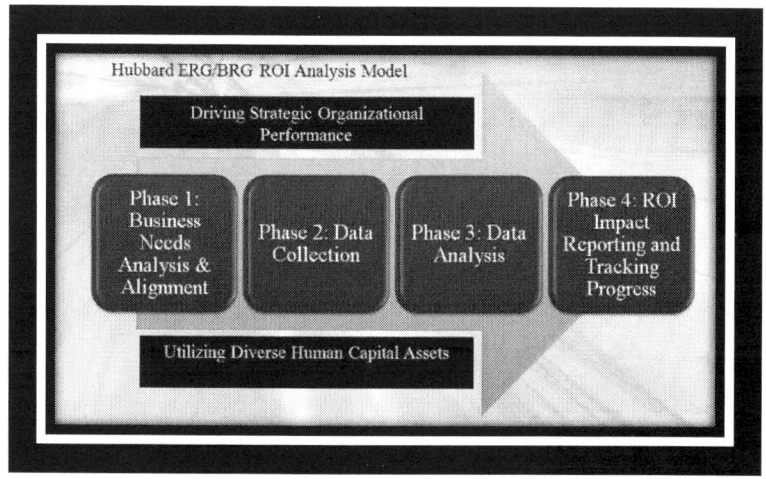

![Hubbard ERG/BRG ROI Analysis Model diagram showing four phases: Phase 1: Business Needs Analysis & Alignment, Phase 2: Data Collection, Phase 3: Data Analysis, Phase 4: ROI Impact Reporting and Tracking Progress, with "Driving Strategic Organizational Performance" on top and "Utilizing Diverse Human Capital Assets" on bottom.]

Hubbard ERG/BRG ROI Analysis Model^{tm}

The steps in this model work together to produce a powerful analytic framework that will help your ERG/BRG structure, analyze, report, and benchmark the results of your initiatives.

The model is organized around four main phases:

1. **Business Needs Analysis**
2. **Data Collection**
3. **Data Analysis**
4. **Reporting and Tracking Progress**

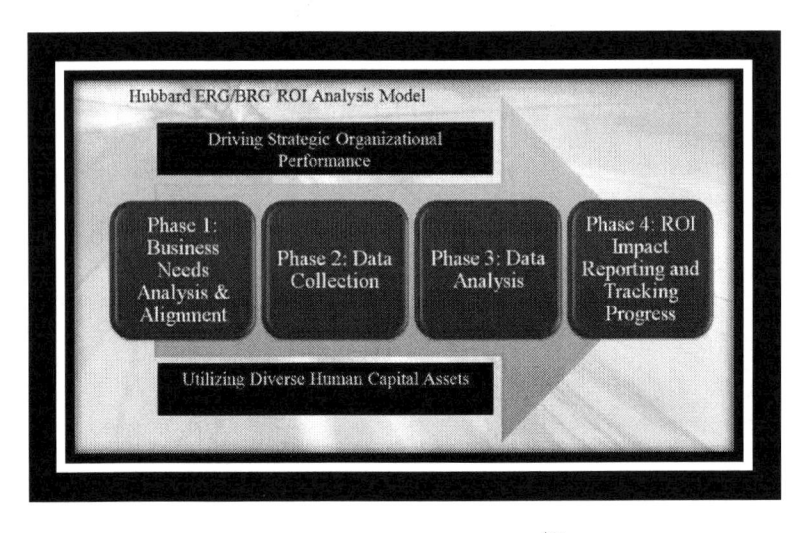

Hubbard ERG/BRG ROI Analysis Model™

Business Needs Analysis

Creating an effective DROI-based ERG/BRG initiative evaluation process requires that you clearly identify what you want to know as a result of implementing an ERG/BRG initiative measurement study. This should be based on, at bare minimum, the identification of business problems or opportunities related to the organization's key business strategy and/or the Business Needs Analysis outcomes you generated during the Business Needs Analysis and Alignment process.

The first three steps of the ERG/BRG ROI Analysis Model:
1. **Reviewing the Organization's Business Strategy**

[Handwritten annotation at top: % / # of women by department by job code]

2. **Identifying Diversity Objectives linked to Business Challenges**
3. **Identifying ERG/BRG Objectives Linked to Diversity Strategy**

combine to produce a comprehensive, systematic alignment and business needs analysis process that serves as the foundation of your intervention(s). You should also be prepared to list a series of research questions you would like answered or hypotheses you would like to test. These questions may include things such as "In what departments or areas do we have the highest level of need that matches the skills, capabilities, and ideas generated from our ERG/BRG members?", "In what diverse customer markets have we trained our sales force in utilizing cultural competencies and multicultural marketing ideas to sell our products or services that enhanced our organization's Key Performance Indicators (KPIs)?", "How has our diverse work team innovation 'Lunch and Learn' workshop improved the operational performance of attendees?", "What was the dollar value and/or number of patents generated by our idea- and solution-generation (creative) process workshop using current cross-functional ERG and BRG teams?"

While planning ways to address these research questions and ideas, it may be helpful to begin with the end in mind. That is, think of what will appear on your research report that will ultimately become an outcome that drives your *ERG/BRG Return on Investment* (BRGROI®) *Report*, create placeholders for them, and then generate the questions or hypotheses that must be answered in order for data to show up on the report as results. The final step in this phase is to summarize the questions you would like answered and formulate ERG and BRG measurement study objectives that will guide your work. Once this is done, you are ready to consider the appropriate data collection methods and develop your data collection plan.

Data Collection

Data collection is central to the DROI® process. A good portion of your data will be collected using "in-process" and "end-of-process" evaluation methods such as surveys, focus groups, etc. In some situations, post- DROI® study data are collected and compared to pre-study situations, control group differences, and expectations. Both hard data (representing output, quality, cost, time, and frequency) and soft data (including work habits, work climate, and attitudes) are collected. Data are collected using a variety of methods, including but not limited to the following:

- Follow-up surveys
- Post-study interviews
- Focus groups

- Short-term pilot project assignments
- Action plans

The important challenge in the data collection phase is to select the method or methods appropriate for the organizational setting and within the time and budget constraints of the organization. During this phase, you will identify the data collection processes and specific metrics to use, create the appropriate evaluation instruments, and apply organizational change methodologies such as the Hubbard Diversity 9-S Framework, which includes Shared Vision, Shared Values, Standards, Strategy, Structure, Systems, Style, Skills, and Staff Diversity (Hubbard, 1999).

Diversity 9-S Framework for Organizational Change

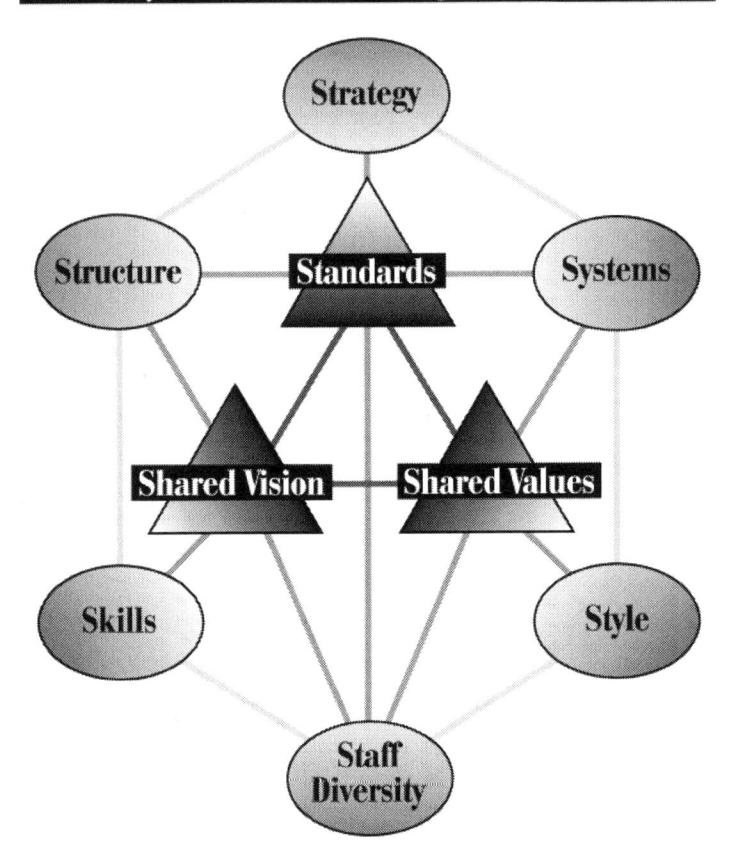

Hubbard Diversity 9-S Framework

Shared Vision

This element is a mutually derived strategic direction among employees, management, and the organization's customers. It reflects the organization's aspirations, purpose, goals, and objectives. It is represented by a visual image of a desired future for the organization to meet the strategic needs of its stakeholders.

When measuring this dimension of the Diversity 9-S Framework, it is important to examine:

- The clarity of the diversity vision for the organization and its key stakeholders

- The presence of an organizational visual image illustrating the desired future state in pictures, images, sounds, and feelings that will be in place once this future state is achieved

- How thoroughly diversity initiatives are being supported, and what can be done to further achievement of the diversity vision

Shared Values

This element requires re-examination of organizational values and culture or the "guiding and daily beliefs." It offers an opportunity to interpret values and identity and bridge any gaps between espoused values and individual behavior. This requires an investment of time and resources.

Top management must make a commitment to ensure that values related to diversity are clearly understood and practiced by all. If the principle values of leveraging diversity are in place and operating, they will be seen in what people do, not what's written in a brochure about your culture.

When measuring this element of the Diversity 9-S Framework, it is important to examine:

- The decisions and policies that illustrate these values
- The rewards and how they relate to stated diversity initiatives
- The values and organizational actions that illustrate their use day-to-day

Standards

This element includes concise, measurable success factors that apply to all aspects of the organizational framework. It provides consistent feedback on how well the organization is meeting its diversity commitments to all stakeholders during and after the transition and change process. The diversity standards dimension is the benchmark of the effort.

Organization systems that are highly accountable require that each system be supported by critical success factors that reflect changes to the organization and its customers.

When measuring this dimension of the Diversity 9-S Framework, it is important to examine:

- The need for tracking systems to be in place and agreed to
- Hard and soft diversity measures of performance in place and valued as evidenced by a visible reward system
- Best practices identified and benchmarked
- "Report card" and/or "mental model" diversity measures in place and utilized to measure effectiveness at the activity, process, outcome, impact and value-added levels.

Strategy

This element includes tactics, plans and integrating mechanisms for business objectives, as well as plans and programs that relate to valuing and leveraging diversity. An organization's marketing, financial, and operations strategies have direct linkages to the full utilization of its human resources.

Effectively utilizing this element in a diversity change effort requires that each organization have a "human capital plan" that is every bit as strategic as the allocation of its business capital. Opportunities abound for organizations that make explicit, concrete connections between the goals of the organization and the effective management and leveraging of diverse workforce resources.

When measuring this dimension of the Diversity 9-S Framework, it is important to identify and examine:

- Diversity work practices that leverage the talents and skills of diverse work teams

- The groups that influence strategy formulation and monitoring the requirements for diverse workforce representation and input

- Formal business strategies to determine if they are built to capitalize on diverse workforce resources to meet competitive and other organizational needs

Structure

This element makes certain that the proper organization structural framework is in place to support an inclusive work environment. Are new reporting relationship structures needed within the organization to convey the sense of urgency, accountability, and importance for utilizing the talents of the diverse workforce?

Are new task forces, advisory committees, or self-directed teams needed to address and direct attention to diversity issues and the way diverse workforce needs are addressed?

Changes in the organization chart and its structure send a loud message about who and what are important.

When measuring this dimension of the Diversity 9-S Framework, it is important to examine:

- Whether operational and team structures are designed to support diversity
- Whether integrating mechanisms exist for problem solving and information sharing using workforce diversity.

Systems

This element includes such organizational components as recruitment and hiring practices, training and development policies, promotion and succession rules, performance appraisal regulations, and compensation practices. Each must be examined to determine congruency with the organization's diversity imperatives.

In essence, all policies, practices, rules, regulations, and procedures that employees follow to perform job-related duties must be examined for possible change.

When measuring this dimension of the Diversity 9-S Framework, it is important to examine:

- How policies, procedures, rules, and regulations are designed to support the diversity change effort
- Whether different modes of decision making, problem-solving, and communication are used to manage and leverage diversity.

Skills

[handwritten: Skills Database compared to % of women by dept.]

This element represents the talents and abilities of the workforce that can give an organization its competitive advantage. The relationship between the skills an organization possesses in managing and leveraging diversity and the bottom-line gains achieved go hand-in-hand.

Leveraging the rich talents of a diverse work group can add exponentially to an organization's quality of output and productivity. Employee and management skills for working in a diverse work environment must be valued as a competitive organizational asset.

When measuring this dimension of the Diversity 9-S Framework, it is important to examine:

- Whether core diversity competencies are in place and evaluated for all levels of employees
- Whether Level 3 evaluation (skill transfer) methods are in place and fully utilized to gauge whether participants are applying the diversity awareness and skills while carrying out their job

Style

This element includes the day-to-day management and leadership behavior that ultimately creates the climate of the organization (in other words, "what it's like to work here"). Style represents a major force that models the priorities of the organization in everyday behavior. It can be seen in how management and leaders of the organization facilitate the process of organizational performance. It is reflected in how people are treated and the level of acceptance of differences that prevails.

The organization's style must reflect a strong sensitivity and practice for effectively utilizing a diverse workforce in pursuit of organizational objectives.

When measuring this dimension of the Diversity 9-S Framework, it is important to examine:

- The degree to which prevailing managerial practices and styles are supportive of workforce diversity
- How current cultural practices support diversity (rites, mentoring, rituals, ceremony)

Staff

This element includes a profile of the employee body or the types of people residing (and where) in the organization. Information about the organization's primary and secondary dimensions of diversity must be known and leveraged.

A typical misconception is that many more women and minorities reside in the organization across functions and at higher levels. Staying informed of the organization's workforce statistics, as well as current and future labor needs will assist everyone in responding to the challenges of a diverse organizational and customer marketplace.

When measuring this dimension of the Diversity 9-S Framework, it is important to examine:

- Whether the employee base reflects the target diversity mix at all levels
- What groups are under-represented
- What staffing requirements are needed to meet national or global competitive needs

Creating an Integrated Picture of the Diversity Effort

All of these elements must operate interdependently to develop high levels of synergy and to provide an integrated view of the organization's performance. The graphic that follows highlights a sample of Diversity 9-S measures which can be analyzed as part of your ERG/BRG intervention strategy:

Category	Measurement
Core Elements	
Shared Vision	♦ *Diversity Vision/Mission Written* ♦ *# of times Diversity mentioned as strategy in executive presentations* ♦ *% change in local and global customer diversity demographic versus prior five years* ♦ *% change in local and global employee diversity demographics versus prior five years as compared to benchmarked leaders in industry* ♦ *Gross productivity % versus prior five year period*
Shared Values	♦ *Diversity Values written with behaviorally specific descriptions* ♦ *% Diversity Values training conducted* ♦ *# of times Diversity Values mentioned in executive presentations* ♦ *Survey rating of values installation*
Standards	♦ *Family of Diversity measures method* ♦ *Diversity Best Practices compiled, taught, and measured*
Basic Elements	
Strategy	♦ *Diversity Business Rationale Strategy Written* ♦ *# of times Diversity Business Rationale mentioned as a strategy to accomplish the organization's business objectives* ♦ *% of Diversity Goals Attained* ♦ *# of Diversity specific goals completed by department* ♦ *# of Diversity specific goals assigned by department*
Structure	♦ *Degree of Variation by Diversity Dimension* ♦ *# of Diverse Work Teams by Strategic*

Category	Measurement
	Result Area
	♦ *# of Departmental or Divisional Differences Represented on a Team*
	♦ *# of Levels of Management Represented on a Team*
	♦ *# of Geographical Differences Represented on a Team*
Systems	♦ *Diversity tied to management compensation*
	♦ *# and Type of Policies and Procedures Assessed for Diverse Workforce Impact*
	♦ *# and Type of Policies and Procedures Changed for Diversity Impact*
	♦ *Absence Rate*
	♦ *Absenteeism Cost*
	♦ *Average Hourly Rate*
	♦ *% Gender Based Pay Differential*
	♦ *Effect of Absenteeism on Labor Utilization*
	♦ *Diversity Performance Appraisal Metrics*
Skills	♦ *Reaction Level*
	• *Reaction Evaluation Tool*
	♦ *Learning Level*
	• *Pre/Post Self-assessment Tool*
	• *Short-answer Evaluation Tool*
	• *Knowledge Change Score*
	• *Skill (Behavior) Change Score*
	• *Attitude Change Score*
	♦ *Behavior Level*
	• *Post Training Survey for Participants*
	• *Post Training Survey for Managers*
	• *Diversity Behavior Checklist Tool*
	♦ *Results Level*
	• *Results-focused Questionnaire Tool*
	♦ *Return-on-Investment Level (ROI)*
	• *ROI Calculation*

Category	Measurement
	• *ROE Calculation* • *Cost-Benefit Calculation*
Staff	♦ *Time-to-Fill, Time-to-Start* ♦ *Cost per Diversity Hire.* ♦ *Source Cost per Diversity Hire* ♦ *Diversity Hit Rate* ♦ *Diversity Hire Referral Rate* ♦ *Diversity Hire Performance Impact* ♦ *Average Tenure by Diversity Grouping versus Former Employees* ♦ *Diversity Stability Factor, Diversity Instability Factor* ♦ *Diversity Survivor Rate, Diversity Loss Rate*
Style	♦ *Employee Opinion Survey - Diversity elements* ♦ *Stratified Focus Group Feedback* ♦ *% favorable responses on Organizational Culture Audit as compared to previous years, other parts of the organization and industry* ♦ *# of Minorities and Women in Management and Leadership Positions* ♦ *5x5 Study - 5 years at level 5 performance* ♦ *$ and % of Budget Allocated to Diversity Initiatives* ♦ *Organizational Mentoring Analysis*

To be effective, the diversity **shared vision** must be embraced by everyone, the **shared values** must be demonstrated in what people do, the **standards** must benchmark performance, the **structure** must be well-defined to foster inclusion, the **strategy** must utilize diverse workforce assets, all **systems** must reinforce organizational behavior that supports diversity initiatives, the level of diversity **skill** must be behaviorally-based supported by a diversity ROI-based competency model, the management and leadership **style** must facilitate collaboration and respect, and the **staff** should reflect diverse individuals well-suited for their job responsibilities. In order for an effective ERG/BRG initiative to make a measurable difference, the organization's "9-S" framework for diversity measurement must be created, linked, aligned, communicated, and implemented.

Data Analysis

Once the data is collected, it must be analyzed for the outcomes it produces and its Diversity ROI impact. Data analysis is an absolutely essential ingredient when you are attempting to close performance gaps or improve organizational performance overall. It is the only way to determine the connections between performance gaps, improvement programs, and cost-effectiveness of the ERG/BRG initiative.

In general, evaluation is one of the most cost-effective activities in performance improvement, because it is the one activity that, if applied correctly, can ensure success. It is often resisted, however, because of the fear that it could document failure. Evaluation is the process that helps ERGs and BRGs make decisions about the value of all of the activities, initiatives, and interventions that were conducted. It is the only process that will give an objective view of the ERG/BRG's progress towards addressing the business needs, goals and objectives of the organization. Without systematic evaluation using a methodology like the Hubbard ERG/BRG ROI Model^{tm}, the group and the organization is left with "wishful thinking" or self-service impressions that are often wrong and sometimes dangerous.

Isolating Diversity's Contribution

For example, an often-overlooked issue in most ERG and BRG assessments studies is the process of isolating the effects of the ERG or BRG intervention. In this step of the process, specific strategies are explored that determine the amount of output performance directly related to the ERG or BRG intervention. This step is essential because many factors will influence performance data after the ERG or BRG intervention.

Convert the Contribution to Money

To calculate the DROI® of the ERG or BRG initiative, data collected in a DROI® evaluation study are converted to monetary values and are compared to the ERG or BRG initiative costs. This requires a value to be placed on each unit of data connected with the initiative.

Calculating the ERG/BRG Initiative Costs

To successfully calculate the DROI® of ERG or BRG initiatives, both cost and benefits must be tracked and calculated in the process. The first part of the equation in a cost/benefit analysis is the ERG or BRG initiative costs. Tabulating the costs involves monitoring or developing all of the related costs of the ERG or BRG initiative targeted for the DROI® calculation.

Calculating the DROI®

The DROI® of an ERG or BRG initiative is calculated using the initiative's benefits and costs. The benefit/cost ratio (BCR) is the initiative benefits divided by cost. In formula form it is:

BCR = ERG/BRG Initiative Benefits ÷ ERG/BRG Initiative Costs

Sometimes the ratio is stated as a cost-to-benefit ratio, although the formula is the same as BCR.

Identifying Intangible Benefits

In addition to tangible, monetary benefits, most ERG/BRG initiatives will have intangible, nonmonetary benefits.

Reporting & Tracking Progress

Communicating Results

Next, it is critical that you have an organized communications plan to let others know the progress and challenges being addressed by the ERG or BRG initiatives. During the development cycle of the communications plan, it is important to identify communication vehicles to use, how and when the report will be created, when it will be delivered, and how to evaluate its implementation.

Tracking and Assessing Progress

Finally, in order to maintain any gains made or benefits from lessons learned during the process, you must make plans to track and assess the effectiveness of your ERG or BRG initiatives over time.

The Role of ERGs and BRGs in Creating ROI

Building an effective ERG or BRG measurement system requires a firm understanding of the role diversity plays in creating a return-on-investment for the organization. An ERG or BRG measurement system lets you do two important things: (1) manage ERG or BRG member outputs as a strategic asset and (2) demonstrate ERG/BRG's contribution and link it to your organization's strategic business and financial success. Although each organization will describe its ERG/BRG measurement process in its own way, a well-thought-out ERG/BRG measurement system, linked to your diversity scorecard, should get you thinking about four major themes:

1. The key ERG/BRG deliverables that will leverage diversity's role in the organization's overall strategy

2. Developing a high-performance work environment that utilizes ERG/GRG competencies as an asset

3. The extent to which the environment is aligned with the organization's strategy

4. The efficiency with which those deliverables are generated

Identifying ERG and BRG Deliverables

To build an effective ERG/BRG measurement system for any organization, we must understand the organization's strategy implementation process in detail, along with its strategic business goals, objectives, and key performance drivers. This means understanding diversity's role and the cultural competencies needed in supporting these elements as part of a larger strategy map. For example, the organization could have profitability goals focusing on *revenue growth* and *productivity improvement*. We could describe the ERG/BRG's role in this process in the following way:

Revenue growth ultimately derives from increased customer satisfaction in all market segments, which in turn is boosted by product innovation and reliable delivery schedules, among other things. ERGs/BRGs can help the organization's sales force, for example, relate to diverse customer service requirements that drive satisfaction and recurring revenue.

Product innovation strongly depends on the presence of talented staff with significant experiences. Through trained, competency-based, diversity-friendly selection methods and retention programs, diversity contributes to a *stable, high-talent staffing deliverable* that helps the organization meet its objectives.

Reliable delivery schedules in part hinge on the maintenance of optimal staffing levels. Even if turnover is low, the organization must fill vacancies quickly. By reducing the recruiting cycle time through more diverse candidate sources and on-boarding approaches, ERG and BRG initiatives can support an *optimal staffing level deliverable*, which can reduce overall costs that adds to the DROI® impact.

Productivity improvement has links to maintaining optimal production and process schedules, which in turn depend on maintaining appropriate staffing levels. Again, diversity assistance in driving recruiting cycle time drives staffing levels that help keep production downtime resulting from personnel issues to a minimum (Becker, Huselid, Ulrich, 2001).

Developing a High-Performance Work Environment

Once the ERG/BRG initiative and other deliverables have been clearly identified, you can begin to identify and measure the primary environmental components that help generate these deliverables. This high-performance work environment system is specifically designed to help drive the organization's strategy implementation process using ERG/BRG initiative deliverables. This could involve, for example, designing, training, and implementing a valid diversity leadership competency model for ERG and BRG members that is linked to major elements in the high-performance work environment system and providing regular 360-degree multi-rater feedback to these members regarding their use and level of competence in applying the cultural competency skills trained during the ERG/BRG initiative. As with any element of an ERG/BRG measurement system, these data can be presented in a variety of ways. The role of ERGs and BRGs and their ability to add innovation, creativity, and insight to business challenges and opportunities is critical to the organization's success!

Alignment with Strategy

The next component in the ERG/BRG measurement system should encourage you to gauge the alignment of the ERG/BRG measurement system with the organization's strategy implementation process. To transform a generic high-performance work system into a strategic asset, you need to focus that system directly on the diverse workforce talent aspects of those drivers. The focus must be on the ERG/BRG deliverables required to create value in the organization, which in turn highlight specific elements of the ERG/BRG measurement system that reinforce one another in order to produce those deliverables. Therefore, specific ERG/BRG alignment measures will be linked directly to specific deliverables in the measurement system (example: training multicultural competencies to reduce transition startup and critical incident costs in opening a new offices in the BRIC countries – Brazil, Russia, India, China, as part of the organization's global expansion). Connecting them in this way highlights the cause-and-effect relationships needed to support the ERG/BRG's contribution to the organization's strategic performance and results.

To select the appropriate alignment measures, focus on those elements of your ERG/BRG measurement system that make a definable and significant contribution to a particular organizational strategy deliverable. These will differ for each organization. Identifying these measures requires that you combine a professional understanding of diversity with a thorough knowledge of the value-creation process in your organization. Remember that these alignment measures will follow directly from a top-down approach. Based on a larger strategy map that you will create in the diversity strategic planning process, you will identify your ERG/BRG initiative deliverables, which in turn will point to certain elements of the DROI® measurement system that require alignment. Therefore, no standard alignment measures can be provided as examples. Instead, each organization must develop a standard process by which it develops its own set of alignment measures (both internal and external) that are tied to its business and mission outcomes.

Diversity Efficiency: Core versus Strategic Measures

As you consider which organizational strategy areas align with your ERG/BRG efforts, remember there are a wide variety of benchmarks and standards by which you can measure the intervention's efficiency. Some of these measures include the following:

- Absenteeism rate by job category and job performance by group
- Number of stress-related illnesses by group

- Turnover costs
- Number of recruiting advertising programs in place by demographic group
- Average employee tenure by performance level by group
- Number of incidents of injury by group
- Time to fill an open position by group
- Offer-to-acceptance rate by group (diversity hit rate)
- Average time for dispute resolution by group
- Cost per grievance by group
- Cost per trainee-hour
- Lost time due to accidents by group

All of these measures can be affected by your ERG/BRG intervention and encourage cost savings. They are diversity operational measures. For the most part, they only position diversity as a commodity and serve as generic benchmarks. The key is to identify those measures that help create strategic value for the organization. Of course, these will differ for each organization because each organization's strategic value will be unique. It is important to select the measures you include in your ERG/BRG measurement system carefully. Otherwise, it is possible to become overwhelmed by all of the potential metric choices. Benchmarking

Final Thoughts

The implementation of your ERG or BRG ROI analysis and measurement system is critical to the success of the organization and the credibility and survival of the diversity profession. In order to be seen as value-added, ERGs and BRGs must become adept at measuring and reporting the right ERG/BRG intervention results that tie their work to the organization's bottom-line objectives. These metrics must go beyond the "number of attendees attending the ERG/BRG meetings" and simple "smile sheet" ratings that don't meet basic DROI® Level 1 standards. By using a systematic, logical, planned approach, and the Hubbard ERG/BRG ROI Model^{tm} process, ERG and BRG initiatives represent one of the organization's best investments in improved strategic performance and ROI.

References

Becker, Brian E., Mark A. Huselid, and Dave Ulrich. *The HR Scorecard: Linking People, Strategy, and Performance.* Boston: Harvard Business School Press, 2001.

Hubbard, Edward E. *How to Calculate Diversity Return on Investment.* Petaluma, CA: Global Insights, 1999.

is fine for diversity commodity activities, but it has no significant influence on your organization's ability to implement its strategy.

Therefore, an approach to creating your ERG/BRG measurement strategy is to divide your key efficiency metrics into two categories: core and strategic. *Core efficiency measures* represent significant diversity expenditures, but they make no real direct contribution to the organization's strategy implementation. *Strategic efficiency measures* assess the efficiency of diversity activities and processes designed to produce diversity deliverables. To make the distinction between these two types of measures, you must trace the links between the specific measure and its connection with the ERG/BRG initiative value chain. An example might be reducing the minority recruiting cycle time. Because this is one of the first steps in helping the organization achieve the strategic objective of stable staffing levels (a key performance driver), it is an enabler and essential to a key performance driver that adds value. Separating the two helps you evaluate the net benefits of strategic deliverables and guides resource-allocation decisions as well as what diversity-related processes generated by the ERG or BRG will best meet the organization's strategic outcomes.

Hubbard, Edward E. *The Diversity Scorecard: Evaluating the Impact of Diversity on Organizational Performance.* Massachusetts: Butterworth-Heinemann, Elsevier Publishing, 2004.

Hubbard, Edward E. *The Diversity Discipline: Implementing Diversity Work with a Strategy, Structure, and ROI Measurement Focus.* California: Global Insights Publishing, 2009.

Hubbard, Edward E. *Diversity Training ROI (Return on Investment).* Petaluma, CA: Global Insights, 2010.

Phillips, Jack J., Ron D. Stone, and Patricia P. Phillips. *The Human Resources Scorecard.* Boston: Butterworth–Heinemann, 2001.

Further Reading

Casio, Wayne F. *Costing Human Resources: The Financial Impact of Behavior in Organizations*, 4th ed. Australia: South-Western College Publishing, 2000.

Phillips, Jack J. *Accountability in Human Resources Management.* Boston: Butterworth–Heinemann, 1996.

Chapter Four: Prepare and Collect Data

Introduction

Once you clearly "know what you want to know", you are ready to "prepare and collect data". Just like obtaining clarity of vision regarding your diversity measurement study direction, the process of collecting data to measure your ERG/BRG initiative results comes with its own rules of accomplishment.

Identify Data Collection Measurement Areas

Diversity measurement is easier to understand when you know the specific results for which you are trying to identify measures. This part of the diversity ROI measurement process will help you identify the ERG/BRG initiative results you may want to measure.

There are several approaches that may be used to identify the starting point for your ERG/BRG initiative measurement efforts. A full range of approaches is discussed in detail in the Hubbard ERG and BRG ROI Institute *"How to Calculate ERG/BRG Return-on-investment"* workshop. In this book, we will utilize one of the measurement point identification options called the "value-added results" method.

Figuring Out What to Measure that is Value-Added

Before we get started identifying diversity value-added measurement points, we'll discuss the concept of a value-added result and how it can help you measure your ERG/BRG initiative performance.

All ERG/BRG initiative measurement will typically flow from either the diverse workforce results, the business work processes which the diverse workforce is using to produce these results (approaches that maximize diverse workforce inputs, processes, outputs and outcomes), or external diverse group contributions and synergies (e.g., diverse supplier and diverse community participation).

Definitions:

Activities are actions that produce results. Attending meetings, talking with people over the phone, participating in a diversity awareness-training program, and solving problems are all activities.

Value-added Results are the products you generate from the activities. They are the diversity-related contributions that add value to the organization and result from the activities. For example, attending a ERG/BRG awareness training initiative can produce the result: "diversity competent people who are aware of the negative impact of prejudice on productivity levels".

There are a number of reasons why you would use value-added results as a starting point for your ERG/BRG initiative performance measurement. These reasons include the following:

> **Strategic Alignment.** It is critical that all ERG/BRG initiatives are aligned with the strategic business goals and objectives of the organization. If diversity interventions using ERGs and BRGs are to be seen as "value-added", they must be value-added to the strategic business goals and objectives. That connection must be solid and demonstrate correlation and causal links in order to show its Diversity ROI value.

> **It takes less time.** Agreeing on the results you produce takes less time than agreeing on the best activities to achieve the result. While there can be many ways to achieve the end result, the diverse work team will usually agree more quickly on the "end" and less quickly on the "means".

> **Collecting feedback data is less costly.** Evaluating activities requires that someone is there to watch the activities happen. Evaluating the results of the activities can be done simply by looking at the result.

> **It focuses on what is really important.** Measuring activity places more importance on the activity than on the results of the activity. Unless what you want is activity, focus on measuring diversity results that add value.

Other ways to describe value-added results are:

- Outcomes generated by the work linked to business goals and objectives
- Value-added contributions
- End results
- Products
- Accomplishments

Below, you will find a few examples of activities and categories that are ***not*** value-added results. You can use categories to organize groups of diversity results, but alone, these categories do not describe diverse workforce outcomes, end results, products or accomplishments.

Non-Value-Added Activities	Non-Value-Added Categories
■ Diversity Training	■ Profitability
■ Diversity Marketing	■ Quality
■ Diversity Strategic Planning	■ Productivity
■ Cost Reduction	■ Safety
■ Innovating	■ People
■ Process Improvement	■ Teamwork
	■ Service

Examples of Value-added Results

This table lists a few examples of diversity value-added results.

Examples of Diversity Value-added Results
■ Productive diverse work teams
■ More diversity skilled executives
■ Increased diverse customer market

Examples of Diversity Value-added Results

sales opportunities
- Qualified women and minority new-hire candidates
- Solved diverse customer problems
- Productive collaborations
- Continued/increased funding for diversity initiatives
- Diversity-friendly policies, procedures, and systems to support the organization's direction
- Solutions to problems
- Reduced absenteeism in women and people of color employee groups
- Reduced turnover rate for women and people of color
- Reduced sexual harassment complaints
- Reduced lost time accidents among women and people of color
- Increased ideas per employee

Examples of Diversity Value-added Results

- Increased unit production performance during a merger and acquisition period
- Dollar revenue generated
- Profit from accounts
- Delivered products
- Diversity strategic plans
- Diversity competent employees

Use a *noun* as the focus of the result statement. This helps to direct your attention towards the result, and away from the activity that produces the result. Notice the italicized *nouns* in each of these examples:

- *Techniques* for improving diverse customer markets
- *Improvements* in diverse work team collaboration
- Motivated and productive *employees*
- Increased *diversity friendly policies*

Use adjectives or prepositional phrases to modify the noun if they add clarity or indicate the intent of the result. Notice the italicized adjectives or prepositional phrases in each of these examples:

- Techniques for *improving diverse customer markets*
- Improvements *in diverse work team collaboration*
- *Motivated and productive* employees
- *Increased* diversity friendly policies
- *Integrated* diversity strategic plans

Do not use a verb as the focus of the result statement. Verbs in the past tense describe a completed activity. Remember, the end of an activity is not necessarily a value-added result.

Use	Avoid
Diversity competent employees	Diversity training classes completed
Women and minority new-hires	Women and minorities recruited
Increased diversity-friendly policies	Diversity-friendly policies written

One activity that is prevalent among diversity initiatives is diversity awareness training. Because "training" is an activity, you'll need to identify the value-added result by asking, "What is left behind after I successfully conduct the diversity awareness training?"

Depending on the situation, you might answer "classes conducted" or "diversity competent employees." We are looking for the value-added result; therefore the best answer would be "diversity competent employees." Classes don't add value, but diversity competent employees are a valuable addition to the organization.

Diversity Value-added Results Method

This technique works best when the diversity organization's measurement study is focused on identifying value-added improvements in measurable goals such as:

- Increasing retention rates of women and people of color
- Improving diversity climate
- Improving the diversity friendliness of policies, procedures, and systems
- Assessing the impact of diversity training on performance improvement.
- Etc.

In each case, the goal is one that can be measured with numbers and the diversity organization or diverse work group is supposed to help move the numbers in the right direction.

Example of diversity results which support organizational goals

Many organizations are striving to become an "Employer of Choice" or appear on the "100 Best Companies to Work For" list. From a diversity standpoint, this business issue is related to a number of areas in which diversity can have an impact. These areas include:

- The recruitment of people of difference (women, people of color, sexual orientation, physical ability, educational discipline, etc.)
- The retention of people of difference
- Reducing the source costs for acquiring these diverse workforce resources
- Creating the training and promotional opportunities for people of difference
- Pay issues related to people of difference (function, level, race, educational background, sexual orientation, physical ability, etc.)

Examining these organizational goals, they can be measured in dollars, numbers, percentages, and anecdotal data. For example, diversity recruitment and retention can be measured in this manner.

It is important to keep the big picture in mind as you start this process. That is, we are not measuring diversity for diversity sake. It is attached to the context of business. You must examine the results that support the achievement of organizational objectives. This can be accomplished by the following:

1. Review the business issues, research questions and diversity measurement objectives you generated in the "know what you want to know step".

2. Next, review the organizational issues, questions or objectives you are to improve and decide if the diversity initiative can affect them.

3. If the diversity initiative can affect these measurement areas, answer the question, "What value-added result does the diversity initiative produce that can help the organization achieve its goal?"

4. Describe these results as value-added and add them to the list of results you will measure.

The first two steps above state that you should examine the business issues and decide if the diversity initiative can affect these issues, research questions, and diversity measurement objectives. The answer is "yes." Because your diversity organization or diverse work team can work collaboratively with the staffing and recruitment department to improve recruitment and retention systems and processes, you can affect costs, numbers, percentages and anecdotal data in this area.

The next step says to answer the question, "What value-added results does the diversity initiative produce which can help the organization achieve its goals?" In this case the answer is:

- Increased people of difference as new hires
- Improved retention of skilled employees
- Reduced diversity recruitment source costs
- Increased promotion-ready people of difference
- Reduced pay disparities among people of difference and majority groups

Reviewing Historical Data

Another alternative for identifying diversity measurement areas is reviewing historical data. Data are available in every organization to measure performance. Monitoring performance data enables you to measure diversity results in terms of output, quality, costs, and time. In determining the use of data in the measuring diversity results study, the first consideration should be existing databases and reports. In most organizations, performance data suitable for measuring improvements from a diversity initiative are available. If not, additional record-keeping systems will have to be developed for data collection, measurement, and analysis.

At this point, as with many other points in the process, the question of economics enters. Is it economical to develop the record-keeping system necessary to evaluate a diversity initiative? If the costs are greater than the expected return for the entire program, then it is meaningless to develop them.

Using Current Measures

When using current measures, be sure they are appropriate to the area you want to study. Performance measures should be thoroughly researched to identify those that are related to the proposed objectives of the diversity initiative. Frequently, an organization will have several performance measures related to the same item. For example, if the diversity organization works with the operations department to improve the efficiency of a production unit, it might start by analyzing diverse work styles. The impact of this could be measured in a variety of ways:

- The number of units produced per hour
- The number of on-schedule production units
- The percent of utilization of the new work style
- The percentage of work group downtime due to conflict
- The labor cost per unit of production
- The overtime required per piece of production, and
- The total unit cost

Each of these, in its own way, measures the efficiency of the production unit. All related measures should be reviewed to determine those most relevant to the diversity initiative.

Convert Current Measures to Usable Ones

Occasionally, existing performance measures are integrated with other data, and it may be difficult to keep them isolated from unrelated data. In this situation, all existing related measures should be extracted and re-tabulated to be more appropriate for comparison in the evaluation.

At times, conversion factors may be necessary. For example, the average number of new recruits per month may be presented regularly in the performance measures for the staffing department.

In addition, the cost of generating new recruits per recruiter is also presented. However in the evaluation of the impact of a diversity initiative, the "average cost of a diverse hire" is needed. This will require at least two existing performance records to develop the data necessary for comparison (the average number and the cost data).

Develop A Data Collection Plan for Performance Data

A data collection plan defines when, by whom, and where the data are collected. This plan should contain provisions for the evaluator to secure copies of performance reports in a timely manner so that the items can be recorded and are available for analysis.

Developing New Measures

In some cases, data are not available for the information needed to measure the effectiveness of a diversity initiative's impact. The Diversity Department must work with the appropriate department to develop record-keeping systems, if this is economically feasible. In one organization, a new employee orientation program was implemented on a company-wide basis for new hires from diverse backgrounds. Several feedback measures were planned, including early turnover (known as survival and loss rates)-representing the percentage of people of difference who left the company in the first six months of their employment. At the time of the program's inception, this measure was not available. When the program was implemented, the organization had to begin collecting early turnover figures for comparison.

Typical Questions When Creating New Measures
■ Which department will develop the measurement system? ■ Who will record and monitor the data? ■ Where will the information be recorded? ■ How often will you collect data?

These questions will usually involve other departments or a management decision that extends beyond the scope of the Diversity Department. Possibly the administration division, the HR Department, or Information Technology Department will be instrumental in helping determine if new measures are needed and if so, how they will be collected.

Hubbard & Hubbard, Inc.'s ERG and BRG ROI Institute conducts a two-day workshop entitled: **"Measuring Diversity Results"** which concentrates on, among other things, teaching participants how to create new diversity measures, processes and systems to support their initiatives. It is designed to give you a foundation upon which to build your diversity measurement strategies using your specific company's data in class. This will enable you to use it immediately upon your return.

In summary, to be effective, a well-thought out and implemented data collection plan is essential to the effective measurement of your ERG/BRG initiative's impact. Demonstrating the impact of your efforts is only as good as the data you collect and the process you use to show its value! By using the Hubbard ERG/BRG ROI Analysis Model you can demonstrate your ERG/BRG initiatives value in a credible, step-by-step manner that drives business results.

Chapter Five: Isolate the ERG BRG Initiative Contribution

Introduction

Once you have prepared and collected the data, you are ready to isolate diversity's contribution. This step will help you select a method to isolate your ERG/BRG initiative's contribution to the organization's goals and objectives. Although there are at least ten (10) different approaches available to accomplish this (such as control groups, trend-line analysis, path analysis, etc.), we will focus on the use of three of them: participant, supervisor, and management estimates.

A Common ERG/BRG Embarrassment

The following situation is repeated often. A significant increase in performance is noted after a major ERG/BRG intervention was implemented and the two events appear to be linked. A key manager asks, "How much of this improvement was caused by the ERG/BRG initiative?" When this potentially embarrassing question was asked, it is rarely answered with any degree of accuracy and credibility. While the change in performance may be linked to the ERG/BRG initiative, other non-diversity factors also have contributed to the improvement.

This chapter explores three useful strategies to isolate the effects of ERG/BRG initiatives. These strategies are utilized in leading organizations as they attempt to measure the return-on-investment in areas such as ERGs/BRGs, diversity, training and development, and the like.

The cause and effect relationship between ERG/BRG initiatives and performance can be very confusing and challenging to prove, but can be accomplished with an acceptable degree of accuracy. However, is proof the only reason we measure ERG/BRG initiative results and performance? The answer is a resounding "NO"!

Diversity and the Double Standard Subterfuge

Diversity and ERG/BRG initiatives are often held to a double standard when it comes to measurement. Disciplines such as Marketing and Finance, for example, are not asked to prove that inflation will be a particular number. The Compensation and Benefits department is not asked to prove that actuarial tables are accurate predictors of exactly when a person will die, yet they base many insurance and retirement benefits on them. Or, what about executive retreats with the top management team? Has anyone asked for proof that spending thousands of dollars to host executives (and often their families) for a weekend of golf, relaxation, and a little business has yielded a specific dollar return-on-investment? I am not suggesting that these activities are not important, only that the same yardstick should apply in all places.

Proof is only a minor reason to calculate ERG/BRG initiative ROI impact. A few, more important reasons you should calculate ERG/BRG initiative ROI include:

- Assessing progress, urgency, and impact
- Increasing awareness, skill, and productivity
- Improving structures, processes and systems
- Discontinuing or expanding initiatives
- Approving ERG/BRG initiatives/projects (if pilots)
- Building a database on ERG/BRG initiative performance and results
- Enhancing management and others understanding and support
- Improving measurement skills of the ERG/BRG members
- Achieving corporate, business unit, governmental, non-profit, individual, and community goals

The challenge is to develop one or more specific strategies to isolate the effects of ERG/BRG initiatives early in the process, usually as part of an evaluation plan. Up-front attention ensures the appropriate strategies will be used with minimum costs and time commitments.

Let's take a look at some preliminary considerations.

Preliminary Considerations

Diversity Value Chain Impact

Before presenting the strategies, it may be helpful to consider the chain of impact implied at different stages in the "Diversity Value-Chain" process. Measurable results achieved from an ERG/BRG initiative or intervention should be derived from the application of diversity skills and knowledge on the job over a specified period of time after the ERG/BRG initiative has been implemented. This on-the-job application of diversity strategies illustrates the notion that it is critical to link ERG/BRG initiatives to performance as shown below:

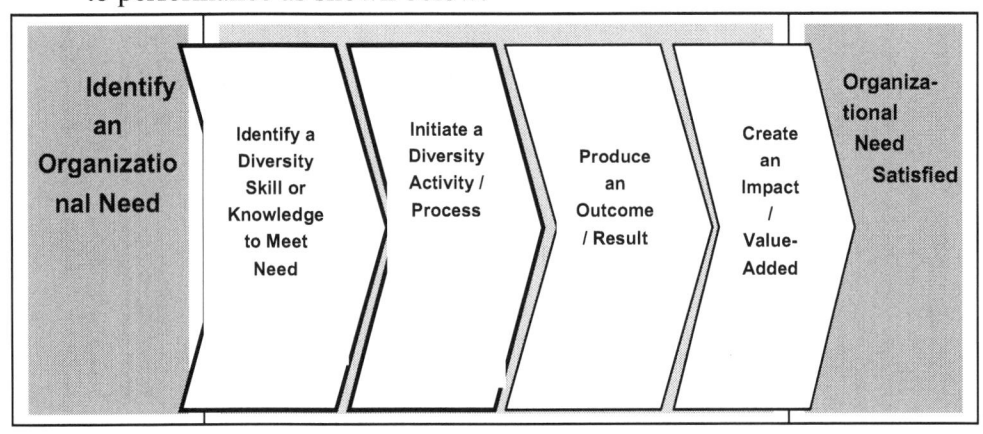

| Identify an Organizational Need | Identify a Diversity Skill or Knowledge to Meet Need | Initiate a Diversity Activity / Process | Produce an Outcome / Result | Create an Impact / Value-Added | Organizational Need Satisfied |

Continuing with this "Diversity Value Chain" logic, successful application of the ERG/BRG initiatives on the job should stem from participants in the ERG/BRG initiative learning and applying diversity knowledge and technologies in a formalized situation to meet a specific organizational goal or objective. Therefore, for an improvement in business results to be realized, this diversity value chain impact implies that measurable on-the-job applications of ERG/BRG member's knowledge & skills are utilized (that is, tasks are performed such as multi-cultural marketing, minority recruitment, bilingual customer service efforts, etc.) using ERG/BRG members collective wisdom and experience generated from their diversity. Without this preliminary evidence, it is difficult to isolate the effects of ERG/BRG initiatives. In other words, if there is no specific learning or application of ERG/BRG member strategies and technologies on the job, it is virtually impossible to conclude that the ERG/BRG initiative or intervention caused any performance improvements.

In addition, it is vital that measurements are taken throughout the entire diversity value chain. While this requirement is a prerequisite to isolating the effects of diversity, it does not prove that there was a direct connection nor does it pinpoint how much of the improvement was caused by the diversity initiative. It merely shows that without improvements at each stage of the diversity value chain, it is difficult to make a connection between the ultimate outcome and the ERG/BRG initiative.

Isolating the effects of the ERG or BRG intervention is an often overlooked issue in most ERG and BRG assessments studies. In this step of the process, specific strategies are explored that determine the amount of output performance directly related to the ERG or BRG intervention. This step is essential because many factors will influence performance data after the ERG or BRG intervention. An example is an ERG or BRG training initiative as illustrated in the Figure below:

Potential Influences on the Diversity Training Solution

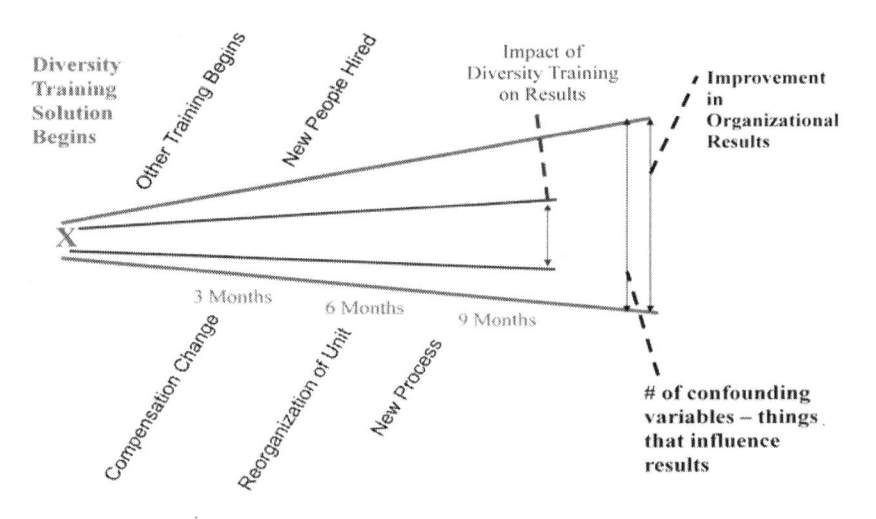

- Diversity Training Solution Begins
- Other Training Begins
- New People Hired
- Impact of Diversity Training on Results
- Improvement in Organizational Results
- 3 Months
- 6 Months
- 9 Months
- Compensation Change
- Reorganization of Unit
- New Process
- # of confounding variables – things that influence results

Figure: Source: adapted from Jack J. and Patti P. Phillips, ROI Fieldbook.

The result is increased accuracy and credibility of the DROI® calculation. The following strategies have been utilized by organizations to tackle this important issue:

- Control groups
- Trend lines
- Forecasting model
- Participant estimates
- Supervisor of participant estimates
- Senior management estimates
- Expert estimates
- Subordinate's estimates (those who work for the participants)
- Identifying other influencing factors
- Customer inputs

Collectively, these strategies provide a comprehensive set of tools to tackle the important and critical issue of isolating the effects of ERG and BRG initiatives. Calculating and isolating DROI® will require an analysis of operational and other business processes to isolate the specific areas where the ERG and BRG training initiative, for example, can be applied to improve business performance. One tool used to analyze the operational processes is the "S-I-P-O-C Chain". This analysis tool allows you to break down operational processes and view them in terms of the way business is done from *supplier* to *input* to *process* to *output* to *customer*. Once all contributing factors have been identified and their contributions calculated, you would be ready to convert the contribution to money.

Identifying Other Factors: A First Step

As a first step in isolating an ERG/BRG initiative impact on performance, all of the key factors that may have contributed to the performance improvement should be identified. This step communicates to interested parties that other factors may have influenced the results, underscoring that the diversity initiative is not the sole source of improvement. Consequently, the credit for improvement is shared with several possible variables and sources, an approach that is likely to gain the respect of those reviewing the results.

Several potential sources can be used to identify the major influencing variables. For example, if the ERG/BRG initiative is designed on request, the client may be able to identify factors that will influence the output variable. Clients will usually be aware of other initiatives or programs that may impact the output.

Participants in the ERG/BRG initiative are usually aware of other influences that may have caused performance improvement. After all, it is the impact of their collective efforts that is being monitored and measured. In many situations, they witness previous movements in the performance measures and pinpoint the reasons for changes.

Organization analyst and diversity practitioners who conduct the Needs Analysis are another source for identifying variables that have an impact on results. The needs analysis will usually uncover these influencing variables. Diversity practitioners must analyze these variables while addressing organizational performance issues.

In some situations, supervisors who are involved in or affected by the performance improvement project using ERGs/BRGs may be able to identify variables that influence the performance improvement. This is particularly useful when the primary ERG/BRG initiative participants are non-exempt employees who may not be fully aware of the variables that can influence all of the systemic performance elements.

Finally, middle and top management may be able to identify other influences based on their experience and knowledge of the situation. Perhaps they have monitored, examined and analyzed the variables previously. The authority level of these individuals often increases the credibility of the data.

Taking time to focus attention on variables that may have influenced performance brings additional accuracy and credibility to the process. It also moves beyond the scenarios where results are presented with no mention of other influences, a situation that often destroys the credibility of an ERG/BRG initiative impact report. It also provides a foundation for some of the strategies described in this book by identifying the variables that must be isolated to show the effects of the ERG/BRG initiative. Keep in mind that halting the process after this step would leave many unknowns about the actual ERG/BRG initiative impact and might leave a negative impression with management and others, since the study may identify variables that management did not previously consider. Therefore, you should go beyond this initial step and use one or more of the strategies discussed in this book that isolate the impact of the ERG/BRG initiative.

Participant Estimates of the ERG/BRG Initiative's Impact

An easily implemented method to isolate the impact of an ERG/BRG initiative is to obtain information directly from the employees involved in the ERG/BRG initiative. The effectiveness of this approach rests on the assumption that employees involved in the ERG/BRG initiative are capable of determining or estimating how much of a performance improvement is related to the ERG/BRG initiative. Because their actions have produced the improvement, participants may have very accurate input on the issue. They should know how much of a change was caused by applying the diversity approaches they learned. Although an estimate, this value will usually have considerable credibility with management because these employees are at the center of the change or improvement.

Let's take a look at an example of one participant's estimations for a particular ERG/BRG initiative:

Example of a Participant's Estimation			
Factors that Influenced Improvement	Percent of Improvement Caused By	Confidence Expressed as a Percent
1. Diversity Multicultural Marketing Program	50%	70%
2. Change in Procedures	10%	80%
3. Adjustment in Standards	10%	50%
4. Revision to Incentive Plan	20%	90%
5. Increased Management Attention	10%	50%
6. Other_____ _____ __	___%	___%
Total	100%	

Participants who do not provide information on these questions are excluded from the analysis. Also, erroneous, incomplete, and extreme information should be discarded before the analysis. To be conservative, the confidence percentage can be factored into the values. The confidence percentage is actually a reflection of the error in the estimate. Therefore, an 80% confidence level equates to a potential error range of ±20%. With this approach, the level of confidence is multiplied by the estimate using the lower side of the range. In the example, the following process steps explain how this calculation is applied:

- The participant allocates 50% of the improvement to the ERG/BRG multicultural marketing program initiative, but is only 70% confident about this estimate

- The confidence percentage is multiplied by the estimate to develop a usable diversity impact factor value of 35%

- The adjusted percentage is then multiplied by the actual amount of the improvement (post-initiative minus pre-initiative value) to isolate the portion attributed to the ERG/BRG initiative

- The adjusted improvement is now ready for conversion to monetary values and, ultimately used in the diversity return-on-investment calculation

Here are some typical questions that must be answered when a participant estimate is considered:

> **Typical Questions to Answer**
>
> - What percentage of this improvement can be attributed to the application of ERG/BRG member skills/knowledge/techniques gained in a diversity training program, from the employee's background and/or experience, etc.?
> - What is the basis for this estimate?
> - What confidence do you have in this estimate, expressed as a percent?
> - What other factors contributed to this improvement in performance?
> - What other individuals or groups could help estimate this percentage or determine the amount?

Perhaps an illustration of this process can reveal its effectiveness and acceptability. In a large global organization, the impact of a diversity leadership and mentoring program for new managers was being assessed. Because the decision to calculate the impact of this diversity training was made after the program had been conducted, the control group method was not feasible as a method to isolate the effect of diversity. Also, before the program was implemented, no specified Level 4 (Kirkpatrick Model -business results level) data were identified that were linked to the training program. Consequently, it was difficult to use trend line analysis.

Participants' estimates proved to be the most useful way to estimate the impact. In a detailed follow-up questionnaire, participants were asked a variety of questions regarding the job applications regarding what was learned from the program. As part of the program, the individuals were asked to develop action plans and implement them, although there was no specific follow-up plan needed. The following series of impact questions were provided with estimations of the diversity impact.

Diversity Impact Questions

- How have you and your job changed as a result of attending this program? (Skills and Knowledge Application)
- What is the impact of these changes in your work unit? (Specific Measures)
- What is the annual value of this change or improvement in your work unit? (Although this is difficult, please make every effort to estimate this value.)
- What is the basis for the estimate provided above? (Please indicate the assumptions you made and the specific calculations you performed to arrive at the value.)
- What confidence do you place in the estimate above? (100%=Certainty, 0%=No Confidence)
- Recognizing that many factors influence output results in addition to the diversity training initiative, please estimate the

> **Diversity Impact Questions**
>
> percent of the improvement that is directly related to this program. (It may be helpful to first identify all the other factors and then provide an estimate of the diversity factor.)

Although these questions are challenging, when set up properly and presented to participants in an appropriate way, they can be very effective for collecting diversity impact data. The following table shows a sample of the calculations from these questions for this particular diversity training program:

\multicolumn{6}{c}{Sample of Input from Participants in a Diversity Leadership and Mentoring Skills Program for New Managers}
Participant	Annual Improvement Value	Basis for Value	Confidence	Isolation Factor	Adjusted Value
11	$36,000	Improvement in efficiency of group. $3,000/month x 12 (group estimate)	85%	50%	$15,300
42	$90,000	Turnover Reduction. Two turnover	90%	40%	32,400

		statistics per year. Base salary x 1.5 = $45,000				
74	$24,000	Improvement in customer response time. (8hours to 6hours). Estimated value: $2,000/month	60%	55%	$7,920	
55	$2,000	5% in my effectiveness ($40,000 x 5%)	75%	50%	$750	
96	$10,000	Absenteeism Reduction (50 absences per year x $200)	85%	75%	$6,375	
117	$8,090	Team project completed 10 days ahead of schedule. Annual salaries $210,500 = $809 per day x 10 days	90%	45%	$3,276	
118	$159,000	Under budget for the year by this amount	100%	30%	$47,700	

Although this is an estimate, this approach does have considerable accuracy and credibility. Five adjustments are effectively utilized with this approach to reflect a conservative approach:

1. The individuals who do not respond to the questionnaire or provide usable data on the questionnaire are assumed to have no improvements. This is probably an overstatement since some individuals will have improvements, but not report them on the questionnaire.
2. Extreme data and incomplete, unrealistic, and unsupported claims are omitted from the analysis, although they may be included in the intangible benefits.
3. Since only annualized values are used, it is assumed that there are no benefits from the program after the first year of implementation. In reality, a diversity leadership and mentoring program should expect to add value perhaps for several years after training has been conducted and implemented.
4. The confidence level, expressed as a percent, is multiplied by the improvement value to reduce the amount of the improvement by the potential error.
5. The improvement amount is adjusted by the amount directly related to the diversity initiative, expressed as a percent.

When presented to senior management, the results of this diversity impact study were perceived to be an understatement of the diversity initiative's success. The data and the process were considered to be credible and accurate.

As an added enhancement to this method, management may be asked to review and approve the estimates from participants. In this way management can actually confirm the estimates, which enhances their credibility.

The process does have some disadvantages though. It is an estimate and, consequently, it does not have the accuracy desired by some managers. Also, the input data may be unreliable since some participants are incapable of providing these types of estimates. They may not be aware of exactly which factors contributed to the results.

Several advantages also make this strategy attractive. It is a simple process, easily understood by most diversity practitioners and others who review evaluation data. It is inexpensive, takes very little time and analysis, therefore it results in an efficient addition to the evaluation process. Estimates originate from a credible source—the individuals who actually produced the improvement.

The advantages seem to outweigh the disadvantages. Isolating the effects of ERG/BRG initiatives may never be totally precise. However, this estimate may be accurate enough for most clients and management groups. The process is appropriate when the participants are managers, supervisors, team leaders, sales associates, engineers, and other professional and technical employees.

Supervisor Estimates of an ERG/BRG Initiative's Impact

In lieu of, or in addition to, participant estimates, the participants' supervisor may be asked to provide the extent of an ERG/BRG's role in producing a performance improvement. In some settings, participant's supervisors may be more familiar with the other factors influencing the change in performance. Consequently, they may be better equipped to provide estimates of impact.

Typical Questions to Ask Supervisors

- What percent of the improvement in performance measures of the participant resulted from the diversity initiative?
- What is the basis for this estimate?
- What is your confidence in this estimate, expressed as a percentage?
- What other factors could have contributed to this success?
- What other individuals or groups would know about

Typical Questions to Ask Supervisors

this improvement and could estimate this percentage?

- Please list the factors with your estimates in the table provided.

The following table highlights an example of results that might be generated using the supervisor's input:

Sample of Results from Supervisor Estimates			
Location	**Improvement**	**Percentage of improvement attributed to the diversity initiative**	**Dollar Value**
A	To reduce low sales levels and customer attrition in targeted diverse customer market segments the multi-cultural marketing and language support initiative was installed. A five- percent increase in customer retention translated into a 125% increase in per customer profits.	50%	$3.2 Million

B	To reduce low sales levels and customer attrition in targeted diverse customer market segments the multi-cultural marketing and language support initiative was installed. A five- percent increase in customer retention translated into a 75% increase in per customer profits.	40%	1.4 Million
C	To reduce low sales levels and customer attrition in targeted diverse customer market segments the multi-cultural marketing and language support initiative was installed. A five- percent increase in customer retention translated into a 102% increase in per customer profits.	65%	$2.8 Million

The questions we asked in this section are essentially the same ones described in the participant's list of questions. Supervisor estimates should be analyzed in the same manner as participant estimates. To be more conservative, actual estimates may be adjusted by the confidence percentage. When participant's estimates have also been collected, the decision of which estimate to use becomes an issue. If there is some compelling reason to think that one estimate is more credible than the other is then it should be used. The most conservative approach is to use the lowest value and include appropriate explanations. Another potential option is to recognize that each source has its own unique perspective and that an average of the two is appropriate, placing an equal weight on each input. If it is possible, it is recommended that you obtain estimates from both the participant and the supervisor.

The advantages of this approach are similar to the advantages of participant estimation. It is simple and inexpensive and enjoys an acceptable degree of credibility because it comes directly from the supervisors of those individuals involved in the initiative. When combined with participant estimates, the credibility is enhanced considerably. Also, when factored by the level of confidence, its value further increases. The following example highlights a combined estimate.

Estimate of Diversity Impact from Participants and Supervisors
Food Service Laboratory Diversity Initiative

Participant	Improvement (Dollar Value)	Basis	% Est. Partici.	% Est. Supv.	Conservative Integration	Average Value Integration
1	$5,500	Labor	60%	50%	$2,750	$3,025
2	15,500	Savings	50%	40%	6,000	6,750
3	9,300	Turnover	65%	75%	6,045	6,510
4	2,100	Absenteeism	90%	80%	1,680	1,785
5	0	Shortages	--	--	--	--
6	29,000	--	40%	50%	11,600	13,050
7	2,241	Turnover	70%	100%	1,569	1,905
8	3,621	Inventory	100%	90%	3,259	3,440
9	21,000	Procedures	75%	70%	14,700	15,225
10	1,500	Turnover	100%	100%	1,500	1,500
11	15,000	Food	80%	70%	10,500	11,250
12	6,310	Spoilage	70%	75%	4,417	4,575
13	14,500	Labor	80%	75%	11,600	11,238
14	3,650	Savings Accidents Absenteeism Productivity	100%	90%	3,285	3,468
Total	$128,722				$78,905	$83,721

Management Estimate of an ERG/BRG Initiative's Impact

In some cases, upper management may estimate the percent of improvement that should be attributed to the ERG/BRG initiative's impact. Management may have additional information and a broader view of the factors influencing the improvement impact on the ERG/BRG initiative. If their deliberations about the value of the improvement are developed in a meeting of other top leaders, then the estimate has group ownership and extended credibility. While this process may be very subjective, the input is received from individuals who often provide or approve funding for ERG/BRG initiatives. Sometimes their level of comfort with the process is the most important consideration.

Considerations When Selecting Isolation Strategies

In this section, we only examined the use of three out of at least ten strategies for isolating ERG/BRG initiative's contribution. Even with these, selecting the most appropriate strategies for the specific ERG/BRG initiative is challenging. Some strategies are simple and inexpensive, while others are more time consuming and costly. When attempting to make the selection decision, several factors should be considered:

- Feasibility of the strategy
- Accuracy provided with the strategy
- Credibility of the strategy with the target audience
- Specific costs to implement the strategy
- The amount of disruption in normal work activities as the strategy is implemented

- Participant, staff, and management time needed with the particular strategy

Multiple strategies or multiple sources for data input should be considered since two sources are usually better than one. When multiple sources are utilized, a conservative method is recommended to combine the inputs. A conservative approach builds acceptance. The target audience should always be provided with explanations of the process and the various subjective factors involved.

Multiple sources allow an organization to experiment with different strategies and build confidence with a particular strategy. For example, if management is concerned about the accuracy of the participant's estimates, a combination of control group arrangement and participant's estimates could be attempted to check the accuracy of the estimation process.

Many ERG/BRG DROI Initiatives Will Generate Large Returns

It is not unusual for the ROI in ERG/BRG initiatives to be extremely large. Even when portion of the improvement is allocated to other factors, the numbers are still impressive in many situations. The audience should understand that, although every effort was made to isolate the ERG/BRG initiative's impact, it is still a figure that is not precise and may contain a certain amount of error...similar to some other estimated business calculations such as inflation, actuarial table estimates, etc. It represents the best estimate of the impact given the constraints, conditions, and resources available. Chances are the ERG/BRG initiative isolation strategies are more accurate than other types of analysis regularly utilized in other functions within the organization.

Too often results are reported and linked to ERG/BRG initiatives without any attempt to isolate the portion of the results that can be attributed to the ERG/BRG initiative. If the overall diversity practice and ERGs/BRGs are to continue to improve their professional image as well as to meet its responsibility for obtaining results, this issue must be addressed early in the process.

Chapter Six: Convert the Contribution to Money

Introduction

In many evaluation impact studies, the examination usually stops with the tabulation of business results. In those situations, the initiative is considered successful if it produced improvements such as turnover reduction, improved customer satisfaction, reduced absenteeism or the like. While these results are important, it is more insightful to compare the value of the results to the cost of the initiative. This allows the initiative to be primed to calculate its return on investment.

Identifying the Hard and Soft Data Contained in the Diversity Contribution

After collecting ERG/BRG performance data, it is helpful to divide the data into hard and soft categories. Hard data are the traditional measures of organizational performance. They are objective, easy to measure, and easy to convert to monetary values. Hard data are often very common measures; they achieve high credibility with management, and are available in every type of organization.

Hard data represent the output, quality, cost, and time of work-related processes. The table below shows a sampling of typical hard data under these four categories.

Examples of Hard Data	
Output	**Time**
- Units Produced - Tons Manufactured - Forms Processed - Items Sold - Inventory Turnover - Patients Visited - Productivity - New Accounts Opened - Students Graduated	- Equipment Downtime - Overtime - On-time Shipments - Processing Time - Supervisor Time - Training Time - Efficiency - Work Stoppages - Lost Time Days
Costs	**Quality**
- Budget Variances - Unit Costs - Costs by Account - Number of Cost Reductions	- Scrap - Waste - Rejects - Product Defects - Number of

Examples of Hard Data	
• Accident Costs	Accidents
• Sales Expense	• Rework
• Program Costs	• Percent of Tasks
• Fixed Costs	Completed Properly
• Variable Costs	• Product Failures

Almost every department or unit will have hard data performance measures. For example, a cross-functional team in a government office approving applications for work visas will have these four measures among its overall performance measurement: the number of applications processed (Output), cost per applications processed (Cost), the number of errors made in processing applications (Quality), and the time it takes to process and approve an application (Time). Ideally, diversity initiatives in this example can be linked to one or more hard data measures.

Because many ERG/BRG initiatives are more heavily related to soft skills, soft data are often reviewed in ERG/BRG measurement studies. Soft data are usually subjective, behaviorally oriented, sometimes difficult to measure, and almost always difficult to convert to monetary values. When compared to hard data, soft data are usually seen as less credible as a performance measure.

Soft data items can be grouped into several categories as shown in the following table.

Examples of Soft Data	
Work Habits	**New Skills**
- Absenteeism - Tardiness - Violations of Safety Rules - Number of Communications Breakdowns - Follow-up	- Decisions Made - Problems Solved - Conflicts Avoided - Grievances Resolved - Counseling Success - Intention to Use New Skills - Frequency of Use of New Skills
Work Climate	**Development/Advancement**
- Number of Grievances - Number of Discrimination Charges - Employee Complaints - Job Satisfaction - Employee Turnover - Litigation - Work Life Satisfaction - Career Advancement Satisfaction	- Number of Promotions - Number of Pay Increases - Number of Diversity Training Programs Attended - Requests for Transfer - Performance Appraisal Ratings - Increases in Job Effectiveness

Examples of Soft Data	
Attitude	Initiative
<ul><li>Favorable Reactions</li><li>Attitude Changes</li><li>Perceptions of Job Responsibilities</li><li>Perceived Changes in Performance</li><li>Employee Loyalty</li><li>Increased Confidence</li></ul>	<ul><li>Implementation of New Ideas</li><li>Successful Completion of Projects</li><li>Number of Suggestions Implemented</li><li>Setting Goals and Objectives</li></ul>

Measures such as employee turnover, absenteeism, and grievances appear as soft data items, not because they are difficult to measure, but because it is challenging to accurately convert them to monetary values.

Basic Steps to Convert Data

Before describing some specific strategies to convert either hard or soft data to monetary values, the basic steps used to convert data in each strategy are highlighted here. These steps should be followed for each data conversion process.

Focus on the Unit of Measure. First, identify a unit of improvement. For output data, the unit of measure is the item produced, service provided or sale consummated. Time measures are varied and include items such as the time to complete a project, cycle time, or customer response time. The unit is usually expressed as minutes, hours, or days. Quality is a common measure, and the unit may be one error, reject, defect, or rework item. Soft data measures are varied, and the unit of improvement may include items such as a grievance, an absence, an employee turnover statistic, or a one-point change in the customer satisfaction index.

Determine the Value of Each Unit. Place a value (V) on the unit identified in the first step. For measures of production, quality, cost, and time, the process is relatively easy. Most organizations have records or reports reflecting the value of items such as one unit of production or the cost of a defect. Soft data are more difficult to convert to a value, since the cost of one absence, one grievance, or a one-point change in the diversity attitude survey is often difficult to pinpoint. The array of strategies offered in this chapter will include a variety of techniques to make this conversion. When more than one value is available, either the most credible or the lowest value should be used.

Calculate the Change in Performance Data. Calculate the change in output data after the effects of the diversity initiative have been isolated from other influences. The change (ΔP) is the performance improvement, measured as hard or soft data that is directly attributable to the diversity initiative. The value may represent the performance improvement for individuals, a team, a group or several groups of participants or an organization.

Determine an Annual Amount for the Change. Annualize the ΔP value to develop a total change in the performance data for one year. This procedure has become a standard approach with many organizations that wish to capture the total benefits of the diversity initiative. Although the benefits may not be realized at the same level for an entire year, some diversity initiatives will continue to produce benefits beyond one year. Therefore, using one year of benefits is considered a conservative approach.

Calculate the Total Value of the Improvement. Develop the total value of improvement by multiplying the annual performance change (ΔP) by the unit value (V) for the complete performance group in question. For example, if one group of participants for a diversity initiative is being evaluated, the total value will include the total improvement for all participants in the group. This value for annual diversity initiative benefits is then compared to the cost of the diversity initiative usually through the diversity return on investment (DROI) calculation.

Strategies for Converting Data to Monetary Values

An example taken from a cross-functional team building initiative at a manufacturing plant describes the five-step process of converting data to monetary values. This initiative was developed and implemented after a needs assessment revealed that a lack of teamwork was causing an excessive number of grievances. This diversity initiative was designed to reduce the number of grievances filed at Step two. This is the step in which the grievance is recorded in writing and becomes a measurable soft data item. Therefore, the actual number of grievances resolved at Step two in the grievance process was selected as an output measure. The table diagram below illustrates the steps taken to assign a monetary value to the data. The total monetary impact of this diversity initiative was $546,000.

An Example of the Steps to Convert Data to Monetary Values	
Setting: Cross-functional Teambuilding Initiative in a Manufacturing Plant	
Steps	**Description**
1	**Focus on a Unit of Improvement** One grievance reaching Step two in the four-step grievance resolution process
2	**Determine a Value of Each Unit** Using internal experts—the labor relations staff and the diversity staff—the cost of an average grievance was estimated to be $6,500 when considering time and direct costs. (V = $6,500)
3	**Calculate the Change in Performance Data** Six months after the initiative was completed, total grievances per month reaching Step two declined by ten. Seven of the ten grievance reductions were related to the diversity initiative as determined by supervisors (*Isolating the Effects of Diversity*)
4	**Determine an Annual Amount for the Change** Using the six month value, seven per month, yields an annual improvement of 84 (ΔP)
5	**Calculate the Annual Value of the Improvement** Annual Value = $\Delta P \times V$ = 84 x $6,500 = $546,000

There are a number of strategies available to convert data to monetary values. Some of the strategies are appropriate for a specific type of data category, while other strategies can be used with virtually any type of data. We will explore a few of these strategies in detail in this section of the book. Additional strategies are taught in the "Calculating Diversity Return on Investment Workshop" mentioned earlier. In general, the ERG/BRG's challenge is to select the particular strategy that best matches the type of data and situation. Several strategies are presented in the next section, beginning with the most credible approach.

Converting the Contribution to Money

To calculate the DROI® of an ERG or BRG training or other initiative, data collected in a DROI® evaluation study are converted to monetary values and are compared to the ERG or BRG initiative costs. This requires a value to be placed on each unit of data connected with the initiative. There are at least 10 different strategies available to convert data to monetary values. The specific strategy selected usually depends on the type of data and the initiative under analysis (Phillips, 2001):

1. **Output data** are converted to profit contribution or cost saving. In this strategy, output increases are converted to monetary value based on their unit contribution to profit or the unit of cost reduction.

2. The **cost of quality** is calculated and quality improvements are directly converted to cost savings.

3. For ERG and BRG initiatives where employee time is saved, the **participant's wages and benefits** are used for the value of time. Because a variety of programs focus on improving the time required to complete projects, processes, or daily activities, the value of time becomes an important and critical issue.

4. **Historical costs** are used when they are available for a specific variable. In this case, organizational cost data are utilized to establish the specific value of an improvement.

5. When available, **internal and external experts** may be used to estimate a value for an improvement. In this situation, the credibility of the estimate hinges on the expertise and reputation of the individual.

6. **External databases** are sometimes available to estimate the value or cost of data items. Research, government, and industry databases can provide important information for these values. The difficulty lies in finding a specific database related to the ERG or BRG initiative under analysis.

7. **Participants** estimate the value of the data item. For this approach to be effective, participants must be capable of providing a value for the improvement.

8. **Supervisors of participants** provide estimates when they are both willing and capable of assigning values to the improvement. This approach is especially useful when participants are not fully capable of providing this input or in situations where supervisors need to confirm or adjust the participant's estimate.

9. **Senior management** may provide estimates on the values of an improvement. This approach is particularly helpful to establish values for performance measures that are very important to senior management.

10. **Diversity staff** estimates may be used to determine the value of an output data item. In these cases, it is essential for the estimates to be provided on an unbiased basis.

This step in the Hubbard DROI® Analysis Model is very important and absolutely necessary for determining the monetary benefits from an ERG or BRG initiative. The process is challenging, particularly with soft data, but it can be accomplished if done in a process driven manner using one or more of these strategies.

Strategy: Converting Output Data to Contribution

When an ERG/BRG initiative has produced a change in output, the value of the increased output can usually be determined from the organization's accounting or operating records. For organizations operating on a profit basis, this value is usually the marginal profit contribution of an additional unit of production, unit of sale, or unit of service provided. For example, a diverse, cross-functional sales team in a major appliance manufacturer is able to boost sales of small refrigerators in multi-ethnic markets with a series of comprehensive multicultural marketing and sales training programs created by a joint ERG/BRG and Sales and Marketing team. The unit of improvement, therefore, is the profit margin of one refrigerator.

In organizations that are performance rather than profit driven, this value is usually reflected in the savings accumulated when an additional unit of output is realized for the same input requirements. For example, in the visa section of a government office, an additional visa application is processed at no additional cost. Therefore, an increase in output translates into a cost savings equal to the unit cost of processing a visa.

The formulas and calculations used to measure this contribution depend on the organization and its records. Most organizations have this type of data readily available for performance monitoring and goal setting. Managers often use marginal cost statements and sensitivity analyses to pinpoint the value associated with changes in output. If the data are not available, the ERG/BRG must initiate or coordinate the development of the appropriate values.

An example involving a commercial bank shows that a multi-ethnic market sales seminar (created by a joint team of ERG/BRG members and the training department) for consumer loan officers was conducted that resulted in additional consumer loan volume in new, multi-ethnic markets (output). To measure the return on investment in this ERG/BRG initiative, it is necessary to calculate the value (profit contribution) of one additional consumer loan. This is a relatively easy item to calculate from bank records. The following table shows several components that are necessary for this calculation.

Loan Profitability Analysis	
Profit Contribution	**Unit Value**
Average Loan Size	$15,500
Average Loan Yield	9.75%
Average Cost of Funds (including branch costs)	5.50%
Direct Costs for Consumer Lending	0.82%
Corporate Overhead	1.61%
Net Profit Per Loan	**1.82%**

The first step is to determine the yield, which is available from bank records. Next, the average spread between the cost of funds and the yield received on the loan is calculated. For example, the bank could obtain funds from depositors at 5.5% on average, including the cost of operating the branches. The direct costs of making the loan, such as salaries of employees directly involved in consumer lending and advertising costs in current and new ethnic markets for consumer loans, has to be subtracted from the difference. When conducting a historical analysis of costs, these direct costs amounted to 0.82% of the loan value. To cover overhead costs for other corporate functions, an additional 1.61% was subtracted from the value. The remaining 1.82% of the average loan value represented the bank's profit margin on a loan. These are just a few examples to demonstrate methods used in converting output data to contribution strategy. Let's examine another strategy.

Strategy: Calculating the Cost of Quality

Quality is a critical issue, and its costs are an important issue in most manufacturing and service firms. Since some ERG/BRG initiatives can be designed to improve quality, the ERG/BRG must increase its understanding of and place a high value on improving certain quality measures. For some quality measures, the task is easy. For example, if quality is measured with a defect rate, the value of the improvement is the cost to repair or replace the product. The most obvious cost of poor quality is the scrap or waste generated by mistakes, poor communication, or conflicts in work style. Defective products, spoiled raw materials, and discarded paperwork are all results of poor quality. This scrap and waste translates directly into monetary value. For example, in a production environment, the costs of a defective product are the total cost incurred up to the point the mistake is identified minus the salvage value.

Employee mistakes and errors can cause expensive rework. The most costly rework occurs when a product is delivered to a customer and must be returned for correction. The cost of rework includes both labor and direct costs. In some organizations, the cost of rework can be as much as 35% of operating costs. Perhaps the costliest element of poor quality is customer and client dissatisfaction. In some cases, serious mistakes can result in lost business. Customer dissatisfaction is difficult to quantify, and attempts to arrive at a monetary value may be impossible using direct methods. Usually the judgment and expertise of sales, marketing, or quality managers or someone who is familiar with the customer market's behavior when dissatisfaction occurs are the best sources by which to try to measure the impact of dissatisfaction. A growing number of quality experts are measuring customer and client dissatisfaction with market surveys. However, other strategies discussed in this chapter may be more appropriate to measure the cost of customer dissatisfaction.

Strategy: Converting Employee Time

Reduction in employee time is a common objective for an ERG/BRG initiative's impact on organizational performance. In a team environment, an ERG/BRG initiative focused on the development of diverse, cross-functional teamwork skills could enable a team to perform a task in a shorter time frame, or with fewer people. The most obvious time savings are from labor reduction costs in performing work. The monetary savings is found by multiplying the hours saved times the labor cost per hour. For example, if after attending an ERG/BRG teambuilding workshop, participants estimate they each save an average of 74 minutes per day, worth $31.25 per day or $7,500 per year (240 work days times $31.25), then this is an added value to the organization. This timesaving is based on the average salary plus benefits for the typical participant. If the program has 25 participants, then the total annual savings is $187,500.

The average wage with a percent added for employee benefits will suffice for most calculations. However, employee time may be worth more. For example, additional costs in maintaining an employee (office space, furniture, telephone, utilities, computers, secretarial support, and other overhead expenses) could be included in the average labor cost. Therefore, the average wage rate may quickly grow to a large number. However, the conservative approach is to use the salary plus employee benefits method. In addition to the labor cost per hour, other benefits can result from a timesaving. These include improved service, avoidance of penalties for late projects, and the creation of additional opportunities for profit. These values can be estimated using other methods.

A word of caution is in order when time savings are developed. Time saving is only realized when the amount of time saved translates into a cost reduction or profit contribution. If an ERG/BRG initiative results in a savings in employee's time, a monetary value is realized only if the employee used the additional time in a productive way. If an ERG/BRG's cross-functional team-based program generates a new process that eliminates several hours of work each day, the actual savings will be realized only if there is a cost savings from a reduction in employees or a reduction in overtime pay. Therefore, an important preliminary step in developing time savings is to determine if a "true" saving will be realized.

Strategy: Using Historical Costs

Sometimes historical records contain the value of a measure and reflect the cost (or value) of a unit of improvement. This strategy involves identifying the appropriate records and tabulating the actual cost components for the item in question. For example, a large construction firm implemented an ERG/BRG initiative to improve safety performance. The program improved several safety-related performance measures ranging from OSHA fines to total worker compensation costs. Examining the company's records using one year of data, ERG/BRG members calculated the average cost for each safety measure.

Historical data are usually available for most hard data. Unfortunately, this is generally not true for soft data, and thus, other strategies must be employed to convert the data to monetary values.

Strategy: Using Internal and External Experts' Input

When faced with converting soft data items for which historical records are not available, it might be feasible to consider input from experts on the processes. With this approach, internal experts provide the cost (or value) of one unit of improvement. Those individuals who have knowledge of the situation and the respect of the management group are often the best prospects for expert input. These experts must understand the processes and be willing to provide estimates as well as the assumptions used in arriving at the estimate. When requesting input from these individuals, it is best to explain the full scope of what is needed, providing as many specifics as possible. Most experts have their own methodology to develop this value.

Using the earlier example of the teambuilding initiative that was designed to reduce the number of grievances filed at Step two, we can illustrate how an expert's help may be necessary. Remember, Step two is the step in which the grievance is recorded in writing and becomes a measurable soft data item. Except for actual cost settlements and direct external costs, what if the organization had no records of the total costs of grievances (i.e., there is no data for the time required to resolve a grievance). In this case, an estimate would be needed from an expert. The manager of labor relations, who had credibility with senior management and thorough knowledge of the grievance process, provided an estimate of the cost. She based her cost estimate on the average settlement when a grievance was lost, the direct cost related to the grievances (arbitration, legal fees, printing, and research), the estimated amount of the supervisory, staff, and employee time associated with the grievance, and a factor for reduced morale. The internal estimate, although not a precise figure, was appropriate for this analysis and had adequate credibility with management.

When internal experts are not available, external experts are recruited. External experts must be selected based on their experience with the unit of measure. Fortunately, many experts are available who work directly with important measures such as employee attitudes, customer satisfaction, turnover, absenteeism, grievances, new markets and the like. They are often willing to provide estimates of the cost (or value) of these items. Because the credibility of the value is directly related to his or her reputation, the credibility and reputation of the expert are critical. This need to periodically use internal and external experts highlights the advantages of a diverse, cross-functional team working together on an ERG/BRG return on investment study.

Selecting the Appropriate Strategy

There are many strategies available to convert the contribution to money. The real challenge is selecting the most appropriate strategy to meet the needs of the situation. The following guidelines can help determine the proper selection.

Use the Strategy Appropriate for the Type of Data. Some strategies are designed specifically for hard data, while others are more appropriate for soft data. Consequently, the actual type of data will often dictate the strategy. Hard data, while always preferred, are not always available. Soft data are often required and therefore must be addressed with the appropriate strategy.

Move from the Most Accurate to the Least Accurate Strategies. The selected strategies presented in this section are presented in the order of accuracy and credibility, beginning with the most credible. Working down the list, each strategy should be considered for its feasibility in the situation. The strategy with the most accuracy is recommended, if it is feasible.

Consider Availability and Convenience When Selecting Strategies. Sometimes the availability of a particular source of data will drive the selection. In other situations, the convenience of a technique may be an important factor in selecting the strategy.

When Estimates are Sought, Use the Source who has the Broadest Perspective on the Issue. The person providing an estimate must be knowledgeable on the processes and the issues surrounding the value of the data.

Use Multiple Strategies When Feasible. Sometimes it is helpful to have more than one strategy for obtaining a value for the data. When multiple sources are available, more than one source should be used to serve as a comparison or provide another perspective. When multiple sources are used, the data must be integrated using a convenient decision rule such as the lowest value. This is preferred because of the conservative nature of the lowest value.

Minimize the Amount of Time Required to Select and Implement the Appropriate Strategy. As a rule, it is important to keep the time invested to select the strategy as low as possible. This helps to make certain the total time and effort for the

ERG/BRG ROI study does not become excessive. Some strategies can be implemented with less time than others. Too much time at this step can dampen an otherwise enthusiastic attitude about the process. Remember, ERG/BRG initiatives are often held to a double standard and excessive scrutiny which can cause your ERG/BRG members to be overly cautious about this process.

Accuracy and Credibility of the Data

The Credibility Problem

The strategies presented in this chapter assume that each data item collected and linked with your ERG/BRG initiative can be converted to a monetary value. Although estimates can be developed using one or more strategies, the process of converting data to monetary values may lose credibility with the target audience, who may doubt its use in analysis. Very subjective data, such as change in employee morale or a reduction in the number of employee conflicts, are challenging to convert to monetary values. The key question for this determination is this: "Could these results be presented to senior management with confidence?" If the process does not meet this credibility test, the data should not be converted to monetary values and instead listed as an intangible benefit. Other data, particularly hard data items, could be used in the ERG/BRG initiative ROI calculation, leaving the very subjective data as intangible improvements.

The accuracy of data and the credibility of the conversion process are important concerns. ERG/BRG members sometimes avoid converting data because of these issues. They are more comfortable in reporting that an ERG/BRG initiative resulted in reducing absenteeism from 6% to 4% without attempting to place a value on the improvement. They assume that each person receiving the information will place a value on the absenteeism reduction. Unfortunately, the target audience may know little about the cost of absenteeism and will usually underestimate the actual value of the improvement. Consequently, there should be some attempt to include this conversion in the diversity return on investment calculation.

How the Credibility of Data is Influenced

When ERG/BRG initiative ROI data are presented to selected target audiences, data credibility may be an issue. The degree to which the target audience will believe the data will be influenced by the following factors:

Influence Factors	
Reputation of the source data	The actual source of the data represents the first credibility issue. How credible is the individual or groups providing the data? Do they understand the issues? Are they knowledgeable of all of the processes? The target audience will often place more credibility on the data obtained from those who are closest to the source of the actual improvement or change.
Reputation of the source of the study	The target audience scrutinizes the reputation of the individual, group, or organization presenting the data. Do they have a history of providing accurate reports? Are they unbiased with their analyses? Are they fair in their presentation? Answers to these and other questions will form an impression about the reputation.

Influence Factors	
Motives of the evaluators	Do the individuals presenting the data have an ax to grind? Do they have a personal interest in creating a favorable or unfavorable result? These issues will cause the target audience to examine the motive of those who have conducted the study.
Methodology of the study	The audience will want to know specifically how the research was conducted, how the calculations were made, what steps were followed, what processes were used, etc. A lack of information on the methodology will cause the audience to become suspicious of the results.
Assumptions made in the analysis	In many ERG/BRG return on investment studies, assumptions are made on the calculations and conclusions. What are the assumptions? Are they

	Influence Factors
	standard? How do they compare with other assumptions in other studies? When assumptions are omitted, the audience will substitute their own, often unfavorable assumptions.
Realism of the outcome data	Impressive ERG/BRG initiative ROI values could cause problems. When outcomes appear to be unrealistic, it may be difficult for the target audience to believe them. Huge claims often fall on deaf ears, causing reports to be thrown away before they are reviewed in detail.
Type of data	The target audience will usually have a preference for hard data. They are seeking business performance data tied to output, quality, costs, and time. These measures are usually easily understood and relate closely to organizational

	Influence Factors
	performance. On the other hand, soft data may be reviewed suspiciously from the outset. Many senior managers are concerned about the soft nature and limitations of the data included in the analysis.
Scope of analysis	Is the scope of the analysis very narrow? Does it involve just one group or all of the employees in the organization? Limiting the ERG/BRG ROI study to a small group or a series of groups of employees makes the process more accurate.

Collectively, these factors will influence the credibility of the diversity ROI study and provide a framework from which to develop your diversity ROI study report. Therefore, when you are considering each of the issues, the following key points are suggested:

- Use the most credible and reliable sources for your estimates

- Present the material in an unbiased way

- Fully explain the methodology used throughout the process, preferably in a step-by-step manner.

- Define the assumptions made in the analysis, and compare them to assumptions made in similar studies.

- Consider factoring or adjusting output values when they appear to be unrealistic to a conservative level

- Use hard data whenever possible and combine with soft data if available.

- Keep the scope of the analysis very narrow. Conduct the impact with one or more groups or participants.

Making Adjustments

Two potential adjustments should be considered before finalizing the monetary value. In some organizations where soft data are used and values are derived with imprecise methods, senior executives are sometimes offered the opportunity to review and approve the data. Because of the subjective nature of this process, management may factor (reduce) the data such that the final results are more credible.

The other adjustment concerns the time value of money. Since an investment in an ERG/BRG initiative is made at one time period and the return is realized in a later time period, a few organizations adjust the program benefits to reflect the time value of money, using discounted cash flow techniques. The actual monetary benefits of the program are adjusted for this time period. The amount of this adjustment, however, is usually small compared with the typical benefits realized from ERG/BRG initiatives and interventions.

ERG/BRGs must go beyond simply reporting general reactions to their initiatives as evidence of the initiative's progress. ERG/BRGs must help take the additional steps to complete the following tasks:

- Integrate diversity into business operations

- Track and measure their ERG/BRG initiative results in quantitative and qualitative terms

- Report changes in business performance

- And convert business results data to monetary values and compare them to program costs as a means to compute benefit-to-cost ratios and diversity return on investment percentages

When this is done effectively, your ERG/BRG initiatives will be set on par with other strategic business initiatives.

Chapter Seven: Calculating the Effectiveness and ROI Value Impact of ERGs and BRGs Initiatives

Introduction

Taking the time to calculate the costs and benefits of an ERG/BRG initiative is an essential step in developing the Diversity Return on Investment calculation since it represents the denominator in the DROI formula. It is equally critical to pay attention to both the costs and benefits of any ERG/BRG initiative that you put in place. In practice, however, the costs are often more easily captured than benefits. This chapter of the book highlights some specific methods for accumulating and calculating costs, outlining the specific costs that should be captured, identifying benefits as well as identifying the steps to perform a DROI calculation.

Strategies for Accumulating and Calculating Costs

Importance of Costs

Capturing costs is challenging because the figures must be accurate, reliable and realistic. Although most organizations develop costs with a lot less difficulty than developing the economic value of the benefits, calculating the true cost and benefits of an ERG/BRG initiative can be difficult. And of course, this affects the Diversity Return on Investment. On the cost side, the total ERG/BRG budget is usually a number that is easily developed, however, determining the specific costs of an ERG/BRG initiative, including related indirect costs, and its benefits can be far more elusive. To develop a realistic DROI, costs must be accurate and credible. Otherwise, the painstaking difficulty and attention to benefits will be wasted because of inadequate or inaccurate costs.

Today there is more pressure than ever before to report all initiative costs or what is commonly referred to as fully loaded costs. This takes the cost profile beyond the direct cost of ERG/BRG initiatives and includes the time all participants are involved in developing and participating in the initiative, including all costs, benefits, and other overhead. Taking the conservative approach to calculate diversity return on investment, you should plan to report fully loaded costs. With this approach, all costs that can be identified and linked to a particular ERG/BRG initiative are included. The philosophy is simple: When in doubt in the denominator, put it in (i.e., if it is questionable whether a cost should be included, the rule suggests that it should be included, even if the organizational costs guidelines don't require it). When Diversity ROI (DROI®) is reported to your target audiences, it should withstand even the closest scrutiny in terms of its accuracy and credibility. The only way to meet this test is to ensure that all costs are included.

The Impact of Reporting Costs without Benefits

It is dangerous to communicate the costs of ERG/BRG initiatives without presenting the corresponding benefits. Unfortunately, many organizations have fallen into this trap. Because costs can be easily collected, they are presented to management in all types of ingenious ways such as cost of the initiative, cost per diversity hire, and cost per diversity training hour and the like. While these may be helpful for efficiency comparisons, it may present a real problem if they are presented without the benefit side of the story. When executives review ERG/BRG initiative costs, a logical question comes to mind: What benefit was received for this investment in the ERG/BRG's actions? This can be a typical management reaction, particularly when costs are perceived to be very high. Some organizations have adopted a policy of not communicating ERG/BRG initiatives costs data unless the benefits can be captured and presented along with the costs. Even if the benefit data are subjective and intangible, they are included with the cost data. This helps keep balance when ERG/BRG efforts are viewed by others.

Typical Cost Categories

One of the most important tasks you must complete is to define which specific costs are included in the tabulation of costs in your ERG/BRG initiative. This task involves decisions that will be made by ERG/BRG members and usually approved by management. If appropriate, the finance and accounting staff may need to approve the list. The following table shows the recommended cost categories for a fully loaded, conservative approach to estimating costs. Each category is described in the paragraphs that follow.

Diversity Initiative Cost Categories		
Cost Item	*Prorated*	*Expensed*
Needs Assessment		
Design and Development	X	
Acquisition	X	
Delivery Internal	X	
• Salaries/Benefits-Facilitators/Diversity Council Members		X
• Materials and Fees		X
• Travel/Lodging/Meals		X
• Facilities		X
• Salaries/Benefits-Participants		X
• Contact Time		X
• Travel Time		X
• Preparation Time		X
Evaluation		
Overhead/Diversity Department		X

Prorated vs. Direct Costs

Usually all costs related to an ERG/BRG initiative or project are captured and expensed to that initiative or project. However, three categories are usually prorated over several sessions of the same project or initiative. Needs assessment, design and development, and acquisition are all significant costs that should be prorated over a basic shelf life of the ERG/BRG initiative. With a conservative approach, the shelf life of an ERG/BRG initiative should be very short. Some organizations consider one year of operation, others may consider two or three years. If there is some question about the specific time period to be used in the proration formula, the finance and accounting staff should be consulted.

A brief example will illustrate the proration for development costs. In a large industrial organization, an ERG/BRG initiative was created to improve multicultural teamwork and innovation at a cost of $98,000. The ERG/BRG initiative's development team anticipated that the project would have a three-year life cycle before it would have to be updated. The revision costs at the end of the three years were estimated to be about one-half of the original development costs, or $49,000. The ERG/BRG project would be conducted with 25 groups in a three-year period, with a DROI calculation planned for one specific group. Since the project would have one-half of its residual value at the end of three years, one-half of the cost should be written off for this three-year period. Thus, the $49,000, representing half of the development costs, would be spread over the 25 groups as a prorated development cost. Therefore, a DROI for one group would have a development cost of approximately $2,000 ($49,000/25 = $1,960) included in the cost profile.

Benefits Factor

When presenting participant and ERG/BRG member salaries associated with ERG/BRG initiatives, the benefits factor should be included. This number is usually well known in the organization and is used in other costing formulas. It represents the cost of all employee benefits expressed as a percent of base salaries. In some organizations, this value is as high as 50%-60%. In others, it may be as low as 25%-30%. The average in the USA is 38% (Annual Employee Benefits Report, Nations Business, January 1996,p28).

Needs Assessment

One of the most often overlooked items is the cost of conducting a needs assessment in the exploratory phase of a diversity audit. In some ERG/BRG initiatives, this cost is zero because the ERG/BRG initiative is conducted without a needs assessment (such as mandatory diversity awareness training in some organizations). However, as more organizations focus increased attention on identifying a validated need for an initiative or project, this item will become a more significant cost in the future. All costs associated with the needs assessment should be captured to the fullest extent possible. These costs include the time of ERG/BRG members conducting the assessment, direct fees and expenses for external consultants who conduct the needs assessment, and internal services and supplies used in the analysis. The total costs are usually prorated over the life of the ERG/BRG initiative or project. Depending on the type and nature of the ERG/BRG initiative, the shelf life should be kept to a very reasonable number in the one- to two-year timeframe. Of course the exception would be very expensive initiatives (such as building a daycare facility and its operation) which are not expected to change significantly for several years.

Design and Development Costs

One of the more significant items is the cost of designing and developing the initiative. These costs include internal staff time in both design and development and the purchase of supplies, equipment, materials, audio-visual media, and other items directly related to the ERG/BRG initiative. It would also include the use of consultants. As with the needs assessment costs, design and development costs are usually prorated, perhaps using the same timeframe. One or two years is recommended unless the initiative is not expected to change for many years and the costs are very significant.

Acquisition Costs

In lieu of development costs, many organizations will purchase some diversity programs to use directly or in a modified format. This is often the case with diversity training materials. The acquisition costs for these programs include the purchase price for the instructional materials, train-the-trainer sessions, licensing agreements, and other costs associated with the right to deliver the program. These acquisition costs should be prorated using the same rationale outlined for design and development costs; one to two years should be sufficient. If modification of the program is needed or some additional development is required, these costs should be included as development costs. In practice, many diversity-training programs have both acquisition costs and development costs.

Delivery Costs

Usually the largest segment of the diversity initiative costs would be those associated with delivering the initiative. Five major categories are included.

Salaries of Facilitators/ERG/BRG Members.

The salaries of facilitators or ERG/BRG members should be included. If a facilitator or ERG/BRG member is involved in more than one program, the time should be allocated to the specific program under review. If external facilitators are used, all charges should be included for the session. The important issue is to capture all of the direct time of internal employees or external consultants who work directly with the ERG/BRG initiative. The benefits factor should be included each time direct labor costs are involved. This factor is a widely accepted value, usually generated by the finance and accounting staff. It is usually in the range of 30%-40%.

ERG/BRG Project Materials and Fees.

Specific ERG/BRG initiative materials such as notebooks, textbooks, case studies, exercises, speakers on key topics, and participant workbooks should be included in the delivery costs, along with license fees, user fees, and royalty payments. Pens, paper, certificates, and calculators are also included in this category.

Travel, Lodging, and Meals.

Direct travel for participants, facilitators, ERG/BRG members, or others is included. Lodging and meals are included for participants during travel, as well as meals during the stay if they are participating in education or training-based diversity initiatives. Refreshments should also be included.

Facilities.

The direct cost of any purchased facilities should be included. For external programs, this is the direct charge from conference centers, hotels, or motels. If the ERG/BRG initiative is implemented and an in-house facility is used that represents a cost to the organization, the cost should be estimated and included, even if it is not the practice to include facilities' costs in other reports.

Participant' Salaries and Benefits.

The salaries plus employee benefits of participants represent an expense that should be included. For situations where the diversity initiative has already taken place, these costs can be estimated using average or midpoint values for salaries in typical job classifications. When a program is targeted for a DROI calculation, participants can provide their actual salaries directly and in a confidential manner.

Evaluation

Usually the total evaluation costs are included in the ERG/BRG initiative's costs to compute the fully loaded cost. DROI costs include the cost of developing the evaluation strategy, designing instruments, collecting data, data analysis, and report preparation and distribution. Cost categories include time, materials, purchased instruments, or surveys. A case can be made to prorate the evaluation costs over several programs instead of charging the total amount as an expense. For example, if 25 sessions of a training-based ERG/BRG initiative are conducted in a three-year period and one group is selected for a DROI study, then the DROI costs could logically be prorated over the 25 sessions. Since the results of the DROI analysis should reflect the success of the other programs as will perhaps result in changes that will influence the other programs as well.

Overhead

A final charge is the cost of overhead, the additional costs not directly related to a particular ERG/BRG initiative. The overhead category represents ERG/BRG initiative costs not considered in the above calculations. Typical items include the cost of clerical support, the departmental office expenses, salaries of the ERG/BRG members and/or diversity department staff members (this is prorated if diversity is not their full-time job responsibility, e.g., they have other functions attached to their job such as EEO, Organizational Effectiveness, etc.), and other fixed costs. Some organizations obtain an estimate for allocation by dividing the total overhead by the number of ERG/BRG initiative days for the year (examining how many days they spent or will spend involved in an actual ERG/BRG initiative for the year). This becomes a standard value to use in calculations.

Costs are important and should be fully loaded in the DROI calculation. From a practical standpoint, including some of the costs may be optional, based upon the organization's guidelines and philosophy. However, because of the scrutiny involved in DROI calculations, it is recommended that all costs are included, even if it goes beyond the requirements of the company policy.

Defining Return on Investment

The term "return on Investment" (ROI) in diversity is often misunderstood and misused. In some situations, a very broad definition for ROI includes any benefit from the program. In these situations, ROI is a vague concept in which even subjective data linked to the ERG/BRG effort is included in the concept of the return. The expression originates in finance and accounting and usually refers to the pre-tax contribution measured against controllable assets. In formula form it is expressed as:

Average ROI = pretax earnings/average investment

It measures the anticipated profitability of an investment and is used as a standard measure of the performance of divisions or profit centers within a business.

The investment portion of the formula represents capital expenditures such as a training facility for the diversity awareness program or equipment plus initial development or production costs. The original investment figure or production costs can be used. Also, the original investment figure can be used, or the present book value can be expressed as the average investment over a period of time. If the ERG/BRG program is a one-time offering, then the figure is the original investment.

However, if the initial costs are spread over a period of time, then the average book value is usually more appropriate. This value is essentially half the initial costs since, through depreciation, a certain fixed part of investment is written off each year over the life of the investment.

In many situations, a group of employees are to be trained in diversity at one time, so the investment figure is the total cost of analysis, development, delivery, and evaluation lumped together for the bottom part of the equation. The benefits are then calculated assuming that all participants attend the program or have attended the program, depending on whether the return is a prediction or a reflection of what has happened.

To keep calculations simple, it is recommended that the return be based on pretax conditions. This avoids the issue of investment tax credits, depreciation, tax shields, and other related items.

Sound complicated? It can be, depending on the particular accounting methodology you subscribe to. For the purposes of calculating diversity's return on investment in the "live laboratory of organizations, we will use an effective, simple, straightforward accounting approach.

In this book, Diversity Return on Investment (DROI) is more precise and is meant to represent an actual value developed by comparing the ERG/BRG initiative costs to benefits. The two most common measures are the cost/benefit ratio and the (DROI) formula. Both are presented here along with other approaches that calculate a return.

For some time now, ERG/BRG members and researchers have tried to calculate the actual return on investment in diversity. If an ERG/BRG initiative is considered an investment—not an expense—then it is appropriate to place the ERG/BRG initiative investment in the same funding process as other investments, such as the investment in equipment and facilities. Although these other investments are quite different, management often views them in the same way. Thus, it is critical to the success of the diversity field to develop specific values that reflect Diversity's Return on Investment (DROI).

To illustrate this calculation, assume that an ERG/BRG work-life and family training program had initial costs of $50,000. The program will have a useful life of three years with negligible residual value at that time. During the three-year period, the program produces a net savings of $30,000, or $10,000 per year ($30,000/3). The average investment is $25,000 ($50,000/2) since the average book value is essentially half the costs. The average return is:

Average ROI = annual savings/average investment

$$= \frac{\$10,000}{\$25,000}$$

$$= 40\%$$

Finance and accounting personnel may take issue with calculations involving the return on investment for efforts such as ERG/BRG initiatives. Nevertheless, the expression is fairly common and conveys an adequate meaning of financial evaluation.

ROI may be calculated prior to an ERG/BRG program to estimate the potential cost effectiveness or after a program has been conducted to measure the results achieved. The methods of calculation are the same. However, the estimated return before a program is usually calculated for a proposal to implement the program. The data for its calculation are more subjective and usually less reliable than the data after the program is completed. Because of this factor, management may require a higher ROI for an ERG/BRG program in the proposal stage.

Summary: Calculating the Costs, Benefits, and Diversity ROI Fundamentals

Calculating the ERG/BRG Initiative Costs

To successfully calculate the DROI® of ERG or BRG initiatives, both cost and benefits must be tracked and calculated in the process, then calculate the Diversity ROI percentage. The first part of the equation in this cost/benefit analysis is the ERG or BRG initiative costs. Tabulating the costs involves monitoring or developing all of the related costs of the ERG or BRG initiative targeted for the DROI® calculation. Among the cost components that should be included are the following:

- The cost to design and develop the ERG/BRG initiative, possibly pro-rated over the expected life of the initiative

- The cost of any materials and external staff resources utilized

- The costs of any facilities, travel, lodging, and so on

- Salaries, plus employee benefits of the employees involved

- Administrative and overhead costs allocated in some way

Calculating the DROI®

The DROI® of an ERG or BRG initiative is calculated using the initiative's benefits and costs. The benefit/cost ratio (BCR) is the initiative benefits divided by cost. In formula form it is:

BCR = ERG/BRG Initiative Benefits ÷ ERG/BRG Initiative Costs

Sometimes the ratio is stated as a cost-to-benefit ratio, although the formula is the same as BCR.

Calculating the DROI%

The DROI% calculation uses the net benefits of the ERG/BRG initiative divided by the initiative costs. The net benefits are the ERG/BRG initiative benefits minus the costs. As a formula, it is stated as:

DROI% = (Net ERG/BRG Initiative Benefits ÷ ERG/BRG Initiative Costs) × 100

In other words, the DROI® formula is calculated as:

$$\frac{\text{ERG/BRG Benefits} - \text{ERG/BRG Initiative Costs}}{\text{ERG/BRG Initiative Cost}} \times 100$$

This is the same basic formula used in evaluating other investments where the ROI is traditionally reported as earnings divided by investment. The DROI® from some diversity initiatives is often high. DROI® figures above 450 percent are not uncommon (Hubbard, 1999).

Identifying Intangible Benefits

In addition to tangible, monetary benefits, most ERG/BRG initiatives will have intangible, nonmonetary benefits. The DROI® calculation is based on converting both hard and soft data to monetary values. Intangible benefits include items such as the following:

- Increased job satisfaction
- Increased organizational commitment
- Improved teamwork
- Reduced conflict
- Etc.

During data analysis, every attempt is made to convert all data to monetary values. All hard data such as output, quality, and time are converted to monetary values. The conversion of soft data is attempted for each data item; however, if the process used for conversion is too subjective or inaccurate, the resulting values can lose credibility in the process. This data should be listed as an intangible benefit with the appropriate explanation. For some diversity initiatives, intangible, nonmonetary benefits are extremely valuable, often carrying as much influence as the hard data items.

Cautions When Using DROI

Because of the complexity and sensitivity of the DROI process, caution is needed when developing, calculating, and communicating the return on investment. The implementation of the DROI process is a very important issue, and is a goal of many diversity organizations. Addressing the following issues can help make certain the process does not go off track.

The DROI process should be develop for an initiative where a serious needs assessment has been conducted. Because of the evaluation problems that can develop when it is not clear that a need exists, it is recommended that the DROI study be conducted with initiatives that have had a comprehensive needs assessment. However, I am well aware that in some cases practical considerations and management requests may prohibit this suggested requirement.

The DROI analysis should always include one or more strategies for isolating the effects of the diversity initiative. Because of the importance of accounting for the influences of other factors, this step in the process must not be ignored. Too often, an excellent study—from what appears to be a very successful diversity effort—is perceived to be worthless because there was no attempt to account for other factors. Omission of this step seriously diminishes the credibility of the diversity initiative study.

When making estimates, use the most reliable and credible sources. Because estimates are critical to any type of analysis, they will usually be an important part of a DROI study. When they are used, they should be developed properly and obtained from the most reliable and credible sources—those individuals who best understand the overall situation and can provide accurate estimates.

Take a conservative approach when developing both benefits and costs. Conservatism in DROI analysis builds accuracy and credibility. What matters most is how the target audience perceives the value of the data. A conservative approach is always recommended for both the numerator of the DROI formula (diversity initiative benefits) and the denominator (diversity initiative costs).

Use caution when comparing the ROI in diversity with other financial returns. There are many ways to calculate the return on funds invested or assets employed. The ROI is just one of them. Although the calculation for DROI uses the same basic formula as in other investment evaluations, it may not be fully understood by the target group. Its calculation method and its meaning should be clearly communicated. More importantly, it should be an item accepted by management as an appropriate measure for measuring diversity results. This kind of credibility must be earned by taking the time to complete all of the assessment and measurement steps in the process.

Involve management in developing the return. Management ultimately makes the decision if a DROI value is acceptable. To the extent possible, management should be involved in setting parameters for calculations and establishing targets by which diversity initiatives are considered acceptable within the organization.

Approach sensitive and controversial issues with caution. Occasionally, sensitive and controversial issues will be generated when discussing a DROI value. It is best to avoid debates over what is measurable and what is not measurable unless there is clear evidence of the issue in question. The issue can be included in the overall measurement process as an intangible benefit. Also, some initiatives are so fundamental to the organization's survival that any attempt to measure them is unnecessary. For example, a diversity initiative designed to improve customer service in a customer-focused organization may escape the scrutiny of a DROI evaluation, on the assumption that if the initiative is well designed, it will improve customer service. As more organizations implement DROI studies and standards evolve, the diversity measurement discipline will have increasing evidence that DROI values can be trusted with accuracy and validity.

Develop case studies of your DROI calculations. Creating case studies of your DROI studies can help educate your organization on the full value of your efforts and the benefits in measuring diversity results. These successes and learning opportunities can help other diversity initiatives and other diversity personnel throughout the organization. Hubbard & Hubbard, Inc. offers specific workshops designed to help you develop or turn your existing data into a diversity business case study.

Do not boast about a high return. It is not unusual to generate what appears to be a very high DROI for a diversity initiative. This can open the diversity organization up to undue criticism and scrutiny even when the numbers are an accurate reflection of the facts. The value for DROI will be built as more members of the organization come to understand the processes through their own participation on diversity initiative teams and obvious improvements in organizational climate and performance.

Do not try to use DROI on every diversity initiative. Some diversity initiatives are difficult to quantify, and a DROI calculation may not be feasible. Other methods of presenting the benefits may be more appropriate. It is helpful to set specific criteria for the selection of diversity initiatives that will be evaluated when using the DROI level of analyses.

ERGs/BRGs are a Critical Link for Success

Calculating Diversity Return on Investment (DROI®) of ERG/BRG initiatives is a critical link for success in diversity management and organizational performance. "You can't manage what you don't measure" and managing and leveraging the power of ERGs and BRGs is fast becoming a business imperative. If ERG/BRG initiatives are not approached in a systematic, logical, and planned way, DROI® will not be possible and consequently, ERG and BRG outcomes will not get integrated into the fabric of the organization.

It is your job as ERG/BRG members to make certain that the credibility of ERG/BRG efforts do not suffer. ERGs/BRGs must build a strong business practice reputation using effective Diversity ROI measurement and management techniques such that ERGs/BRGs are seen as a key driver of organizational performance and success!

Chapter Eight: Communicating Your ERG and BRG Success

Introduction

Once you have an understanding of the processes necessary to identify ERG/BRG initiative costs and benefits and the tools to calculate the DROI® impact, you are ready to develop a communications strategy to report it to others. This strategy includes elements such as:

- Considering some general principles for reporting statistical data and results to others
- Creating a Management Summary
- Communicating Background Information regarding the diversity research study
- Describing the Evaluation Strategy
- Discussing the Data Collection, Analysis and Performance Tracking plan
- Detailing the diversity Initiative's Costs, and Benefits
- Profiling an Initiative's Results and DROI® Impact
- Identifying your Conclusions and Recommendations

General Reporting Principles

Reporting the results is almost as important as producing results. It will do you and your ERG/BRG members little good if you are making great progress and few people know about it. In effect, you must become a cheerleader and chief advocate for your ERG/BRG initiative efforts. Regardless of the message, a few general principles are important when communicating your ERG/BRG initiative's results:

- The communication must be timely
- The communication should be targeted to specific audiences
- The media should be carefully selected
- The communication should be unbiased and always modest
- The communication must be consistent
- Testimonials are more effective if they are from individuals with audience credibility
- The audience's perception of the ERG/BRG will influence communication strategy

The communication must be timely - Usually, ERG/BRG initiative results should be communicated as soon as they are known and are packaged for presentation. From a practical standpoint however, it may be best to delay the communication to a convenient time, such as the next edition of the newsletter or the next general staff meeting. Several questions about timing must be addressed.

- Is the audience prepared for the information, considering the content and other events?
- Are they expecting it?
- When is the best time to have maximum impact on the audience?

The communication should be targeted to specific audiences - The communication will be more efficient when it is designed for a specific group. The message can be specifically tailored to the interests, needs and expectations of the group. The length, content, details, and slant will vary with the audience.

The media should be carefully selected - For a specific group, one medium may be more effective than others. Face-to-face meetings may be better with some groups than special bulletins. A memo to top management may be more effective than an evaluation report. The selection of an appropriate medium will help improve the effectiveness of the process.

The communication should be unbiased and always modest - Facts must be separated from fiction, and accurate statements must replace opinions. Some target audiences may view communication from the ERG/BRG with skepticism and may look for biased information and opinions. Boastful statements will sometimes turn off individuals, and most of the content of the communication will be lost. Observable, believable facts carry more weight than extreme, sensational claims, although the claims may be needed to get initial attention.

The communication must be consistent - The timing and the content of the communication should be consistent with past practices. A special communication at an unusual time may create suspicion when a particular group, such as top management, regularly receives communication, the information should continue even if the results are not good. If selected results are omitted, it might leave the impression that only good results are reported.

Testimonials are more effective if they are from individuals with audience credibility - Attitudes are strongly influenced by others, particularly by those who are admired and respected. Testimonials about the ERG/BRG initiative results, when solicited from individuals who are generally respected in the organization can have a strong impact on the effectiveness of the message. This respect may be earned from leadership ability, position, special skills, or knowledge. The opposite of this principle is true. A testimonial from an individual who commands little respect and is regarded as a poor performer can have a negative impact.

The audience's perception of the ERG/BRG will influence communication strategy - Perceptions are difficult to change. A negative opinion of the ERG/BRG organization may not be changed by the mere presentation of facts. However, the presentation of facts alone may strengthen the opinion of individuals who already have a favorable impression of the group. It provides reassurance that their support is appropriate. The ERG/BRG's credibility should be an important consideration when developing an overall communications strategy. An ERG/BRG organization with low credibility may have problem when trying to be persuasive in a communication. Nonetheless, communicating significant ERG/BRG initiative results can have a positive effect on increasing the credibility of the group.

Key Questions to Answer when Selecting the Message

In order for your ERG/BRG initiative report to have the maximum impact, you must answer a few key questions:

- Is the audience interested in the subject?
- Do they really want to hear the information?
- Is the timing right for this audience?
- Is this audience familiar with the views of the ERG/BRG organization?
- How do they prefer to have results communicated?
- Are they likely to find the results threatening?
- What else is happening in the organization that may compete for their attention to focus on the ERG/BRG initiative results?

- Which medium will be most convincing to this group?

To be an effective communicator, you must get to know the audience you will be working with noting how others have been successful in reporting data to them in the past. Find out what information is needed and why. Try to understand each audience's point of view - some may want to see the results while others may not. Others may be neutral. Keep in mind that your reporting approach must reach everyone in a way the helps them understand the significance of the work you have completed.

Now that you understand some of the rules for reporting your ERG/BRG initiative results, let's examine the components to create the ERG/BRG initiative evaluation report.

Developing the Evaluation Report

The type of formal evaluation report used to communicate results depends on the amount of detailed information that is developed for various target audiences. In general, the objective is to keep the presentation to 1-2 pages. For senior leadership groups, it should be condensed in a management summary or briefing. For other audiences, the evaluation report can be "layered" into sections such that you present those portions that are most applicable to your target audience.

The following elements should be covered in a complete ERG/BRG initiative evaluation report:
- Management Summary
- Background Information
- Evaluation Strategy
- Data Collection, Analysis and Performance Tracking
- ERG/BRG Initiative's Costs, and Benefits
- ERG/BRG Initiative Results and DROI® Calculations
- Conclusions and Recommendations

Management Summary

The Management Summary gives a brief synopsis of the ERG/BRG initiative measurement study, the approaches used and the conclusions and recommendations you would like to make based upon the findings. Its basic purpose is to:
- Provide a brief overview of the entire report
- Explain significant conclusions and recommendations

It is usually written last and appears first in the report. Another typical writing convention is that it is usually one page in length.

Background Information

Next, the Background Information section does exactly what it says...provides background information. In this section you introduce the need for the ERG/BRG initiative measurement study and its links to the organization's strategic business objectives. Its basic purpose is to:
- Provide a general description of the events leading to the creation of the ERG/BRG initiative
- Describe the ERG/BRG Business Rationale that links the study to the organization's strategic business objectives. This can be obtained from the needs analysis and the diversity strategic plan
- Discuss specific issues and events critical to the development and implementation of the ERG/BRG initiative measurement effort

This section explains the basic foundation that makes this study valuable to the organization.

Evaluation Strategy

The Evaluation Strategy section outlines the statistical analysis plan that was used during the study. Its basic purpose is to:
- Describe all of the components that made up the total

evaluation process
- Explain in detail the purpose of the ERG/BRG initiative evaluation effort
- Describe the data collection techniques and presents them as exhibits
- Identify other Information related to the design, timing, responsibilities of personnel and the execution of the evaluation.

This allows the target audience to understand the framework that made the study possible.

Data Collection, Analysis and Performance Tracking

The Data Collection, Analysis and Performance Tracking section explains how the data was collected, what occurred during the implementation of the analysis methods, and outlines the techniques and methods used to track the ERG/BRG initiative's performance based upon key assessments taken.

This section usually presents the data collected in both raw and finished formats. And, it illustrates what measures were used that requires special explanations. Converted monetary values are discussed along with the methods of data analysis and appropriate explanations and interpretations

ERG/BRG Initiative Costs and Benefits

This section explains the how the costs and benefits were captured or determined. Its basic purpose is to:
- Summarize costs by examining each cost component
- Show costs as they relate to analysis, development, implementation expenses, maintenance, and evaluation efforts
- Discuss assumptions made in estimating costs

It is important to note that there is no need to explain the complete system for assigning and allocating cost. Including a footnote to explain that a summary description of the system is available from the ERG/BRG is sufficient.

Initiative Results and DROI® Calculations

This is the section of the Evaluation Report that your audience will want to discuss in detail. It is the section that should be crafted to appeal to the informational needs of each audience member. This suggests that if you are presenting in a meeting room, this section should be supported with visual graphics, sound and movement to illustrate the impact of the results such that you appeal to all learning styles—visual, auditory and kinesthetic. This section is probably the most important part of the report. Its basic purpose is to:

- Present a summary of the results with charts, diagrams, tables, and other visual aids.
- Where possible, include a cost/benefit analysis along with the DROI® calculation (DROI® = Net Initiative Benefits/Initiative Costs) and the Benefit/Cost ratio (BCR = Initiative Benefits/Initiative Costs
- Outline various program benefits
- Present a complete picture of both hard and soft data

Conclusions and Recommendations

Finally, the Conclusions and Recommendations section brings the Evaluation Report to a close. Its basic purpose is to:

- Present conclusions based upon an analysis of all information
- Give a brief explanation explaining how the conclusions were derived
- Discuss the impact of conclusions on the successful operation of the organization
- Present a list of recommendations including changes in the ERG/BRG initiative approach or changes to other systems within the organization

It is critical that the conclusions and recommendations are fully consistent with the findings described in the previous sections of the ERG/BRG initiative evaluation report.

While these components are key parts of a complete ERG/BRG initiative Evaluation Report, the report can be scaled down, as necessary to provide needed documentation to meet target audience needs.

Communicating Results to a Variety of Audiences

While several potential audiences could receive the DROI® study, four audiences should always receive the data. A senior management team (however defined) should always receive information about the DROI® project because of their interest in the process and their influence to allocate additional resources for diversity and the measurement of its impact. The supervisors of the initiative's participants need to have the DROI® information so they will continue to support other ERG/BRG measurement efforts and reinforce specific behaviors and methods suggested in the diversity initiative for performance improvement. The participants in the diversity initiative who actually achieved results should receive a summary of the DROI® information so they understand what the entire group accomplished. This also reinforces their commitment to make the process work. The diversity staff must understand the DROI® process and, consequently, need to receive the DROI® study information. In addition, other groups may receive information based on the type of diversity measurement initiative conducted and the other potential audiences.

Other Means to Communicate Diversity Results

In addition to communicating the results of your ERG/BRG initiative measurement study using an evaluation report, there are other methods available. These methods include:

- Staff Meetings
- Supervisor/Leader Meetings
- Panel Discussions
- Management Clubs and Associations
- Annual "State of the Company" Meetings
- Company or Diversity Newsletters
- General Interest Publications - Human interest stories, participant recognition, annual reports
- Brochures/Booklets/Pamphlets/Recruiting Brochures/Special Achievements/Success Stories

Reporting Your Results Should Not Be an Afterthought

Reporting your ERG/BRG initiative measurement results is critical to the total evaluation process. It should not be left as an afterthought simply because you are achieving the intended results. These results have to be communicated in a conservative tone and effective manner to demonstrate and maintain the ERG/BRG initiative's link to the business bottom-line. Your goal must be to communicate the ERG/BRG initiative results with facts, figures and financials that make the business case for performance impact!

Chapter Nine: Tracking and Assessing Progress

Introduction

Tracking and assessing the overall progress of your ERG/BRG ROI initiative is critical for institutionalizing any gains achieved in the process. A tracking system is usually made up of the documents and procedures you used to collect and summarize the data for feedback purposes. Although it is an often overlooked part of the process, an effective diversity measurement tracking and monitoring plan can help keep your diversity initiatives on target and let others know what progress is being made for the organization. By using diversity return on investment (DROI®) techniques, you can establish your diversity efforts on a solid business foundation like any other organizational initiative.

What Does a Good Tracking System Look Like?

An effective tracking system is one that is:

Relevant – The organization receives information directly related to the ERG/BRG initiative measures and metrics being used.

Frequent – Generally, the more frequent the feedback on key items the better. The goal is to provide feedback often enough to prevent the organization from drifting off the ERG/BRG initiative and business performance target.

Immediate – Feedback should come as soon as possible after work is completed or on a regularly scheduled basis once processes are placed in an implementation mode.

Specific – Feedback should state exactly how the organization did in accomplishing the ERG/BRG ROI initiative's goals and objectives. This includes meeting any Benefit-to-Cost ratio (BCR) and Diversity Return on Investment (DROI®) targets as well as stories of success (anecdotal) achieved along the way.

Remember: "You can't manage what you don't measure" and "you can't know if you are making progress if you are not tracking the ERG/BRG ROI initiative results to compare". Unless the organization knows how it is doing in meeting its ERG/BRG ROI initiative targets, it can't improve. Honest, two-way communication between the ERG/BRG ROI initiative implementation team and the organization begins with accurate data about how well the organization is performing relative to meeting its goals and objectives. Without it, both the ERG/BRG ROI initiative implementation team and management can only exchange subjective opinions about how the ERG/BRG ROI initiatives have performed.

Monitoring Your DROI® Initiative's Progress

The initial implementation schedule of the DROI® study provides a variety of key events or milestones. Routine progress reports need to be developed to present the status and progress of these ERG/BRG ROI initiative events and their key milestones. Reports are usually developed at six-month intervals; however, they can be more frequent depending on the informational needs of your audience. Two target audiences, the diversity organization staff and senior managers, are critical for progress reporting. The entire Human Resources, operations communities, and line managers within the organization should be kept informed on the initiative's progress. In addition, senior managers need to know the extent to which the diversity return on investment study is being implemented and how it is working in the organization. To maintain this level of information and reporting capability, automated systems may be necessary.

MetricLINK® an Automated Diversity Measurement System for Tracking Improved Performance

Developing diversity measurement strategies, business objectives and tactics, calculating formulas for ERG/BRG metrics, keeping everyone informed on the ERG/BRG ROI initiative's progress, etc., can be tedious work. Someone must take the responsibility to develop procedures and a method to systematically monitor and track each ERG/BRG measure and set of metrics used to implement the initiative, and then summarize the results over time. This is a task that is best done by a computer or an automated measurement system.

As we stated earlier, there's a saying that goes "If you don't measure it, you can't control it. And, if you can't control it, you can't manage it." **MetricLink®**, a comprehensive Online Diversity Strategic Alignment and Performance Measurement Service developed and operated by Hubbard & Hubbard, Inc., Petaluma, California, has been found to be an easy-to-use, highly effective measurement planning, analysis and reporting system that provides all the information you need to "manage-by-facts". It integrates and organizes diversity measures and strategies all in one place. It is based upon and contains the Diversity ROI Methodologies developed by Dr. Edward E. Hubbard, Diversity ROI Analytics and metrics pioneer.

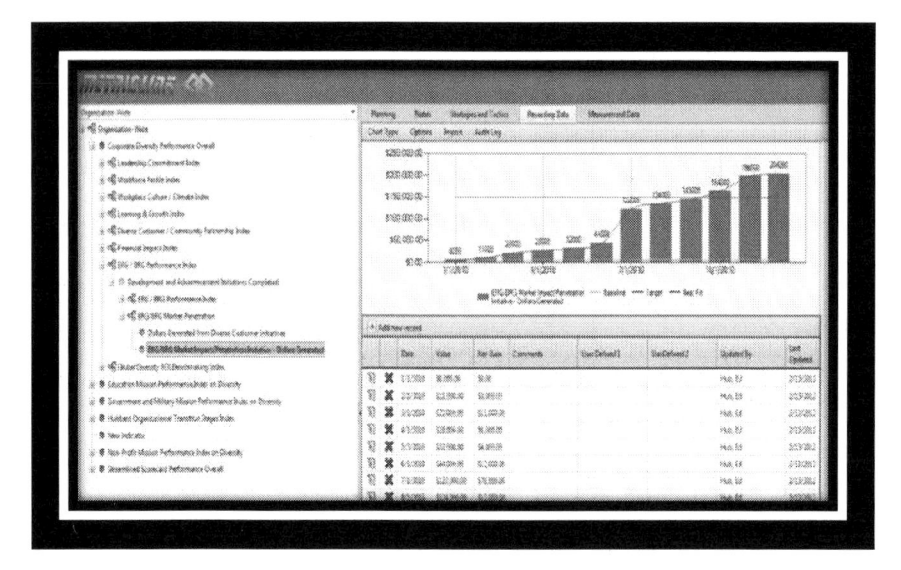

The online cloud-based service frees ERG/BRG members up from some of the time-consuming tasks of tracking, calculating and reporting a ERG/BRG ROI initiative's results.

Some of the benefits of the Hubbard **MetricLink**® Services are:

- Aligns diversity measures with strategic business objectives and the organization's operations structure.

- Multiple views allow ERG/BRG measures to be reviewed in different contexts.

- "Drill-down" capabilities are available to view ERG/BRG measures by component, by location, by workgroup, or by results area.

- Multiple comparisons of actual ERG/BRG ROI initiative performance to organizational targets stretch goals, historical performance, benchmarks, or other reference points is available.

- You can vary target specifications over multiple periods to reflect changing objectives over time.

- "*Weights*", performance scaling, and ERG/BRG ROI initiative indexing capabilities can be used to combine several measures into meaningful summary values.

- Color-coded reporting allows you to easily monitor performance "*at a glance*".

- Team or individual ownership can be assigned for each ERG/BRG ROI initiative measure promoting accountability and communication.

- Customized reporting and printout capabilities are available.

- The Notes, Task and Project planning features are "*built-in*" to capture ideas and actions for the ERG/BRG ROI initiative and organizational performance improvement.

- Easy-to-use menus and icons to intuitively locate features and functions with a "*point and click*".

Using the **MetricLink**® approach, no programming is required and typical administrator training only takes about 4 hours to get you up and running on the system. **MetricLink**® service options allow the use of ERG/BRG measurement templates for key ERG/BRG benchmark measures you can use immediately. Setup and the "ready to use" timeframe is less than a day if standard measures are used and organization specific measures are ready and well defined. **MetricLink**® is Cloud-based offering and can be accessed by members anywhere in the world.

Other Measurement Software Options

Other measurement software options include Survey Monkey, SurveyPro and using popular spreadsheet programs such as Microsoft Excel, Lotus 1-2-3, etc., and project management software programs such as Microsoft Project, as well as using data base management programs such as Microsoft Access or Lotus Approach. These software solutions will however require you to design and program formula calculations, recording and data input elements to track and monitor your progress. Tracking and assessing your progress as the ERG/BRG ROI initiative matures must become a routine, integral part of your system of measurement.

Institutionalizing Your ERG/BRG Measurement System

Institutionalizing the ERG/BRG ROI initiative measurement tracking and monitoring process is a three-part challenge:

- Creating and refining the DROI® process and other measurement systems that supports it; Managers themselves must be instrumental in helping to create the measurement model and align with it. This helps to create buy-in.

- Creating management alignment around the use of the DROI® measurement model; and,

- Deploying the DROI® measurement model so as to build business literacy and trust among everyone that participates in or is affected by these measurement methods.

First, it is important to build alignment around the DROI® measurement process and its techniques: The DROI® model and its measures (Survival and Loss Rates, Stability, Instability Factors,

BCR, DROI® calculations, % of Favorable Responses, etc.) make up a single system. This system must become a cornerstone for management decision-making. Therefore every manager, especially those at the top must understand the system and buy into it. The ERG/BRG ROI initiative must include an effective education and communications component.

Second, it is essential to deploy the ERG/BRG ROI initiative measurement system properly in order to create a sense of ownership among employees and staff. This is more than simple communications.

Thirdly, it is a task of building trust and financial literacy among employees about the numbers and ERG/BRG metrics that drive the business. Unless employees grasp the purpose of the system, understand the economics of the organization and industry, and have a clear picture of how their own work fits into the "business value chain", the organization will never succeed in making the whole system work to leverage ERG/BRG efforts for performance improvement.

Importance of Institutionalizing ERG/BRG Measurement and Tracking

Institutionalizing ERG/BRG ROI initiative efforts is a key business strategy for reaping the benefits of a diverse workforce. It is one thing to have diversity in your workforce. It's quite another to "utilize" diversity as a competitive advantage. To become an "employer of choice" and to meet key competitive realities of the future, the use of ERG/BRG ROI initiative efforts for performance improvement and return on investment must become mandatory.

Chapter Ten: Building an ERG BRG ROI Implementation Plan

Strategies for Implementing Your ERG/BRG initiatives

Developing ERG/BRG initiatives and actually implementing them are two different things. It requires a planned, strategic approach that involves all levels within the organization. This chapter explains how to build the acceptance element of your ERG/BRG initiatives, that is, how to be disciplined in applying lessons of change management to the implementation of the ERG/BRG initiatives you develop. It serves less as a road map to what is contained in an ERG/BRG initiative and more as a guide to implementing the ERG/BRG initiatives.

Diversity is not a program; it is a process of systemic organizational change. Nobody will be "finished with diversity". There will always be people with differences and situations in the workplace that require a poly-ocular view for resolution and performance. And, because ERG/BRG initiatives are designed to drive results, they involve change (both personal and organizational change). Those implementing ERG/BRG initiatives must be change masters who understand how people react to change with their differences. Change involves "exchange". In order to get something, you must give up something. In many cases, the ERG/BRG initiatives require that people in the organization give up old notions of what they used to do as a process or approach, and begin to view those processes and approaches in a business and performance context that make using ERG/BRG initiatives a competitive advantage. Having high-quality ERG/BRG initiatives is not enough to ensure success. Without *acceptance,* this ERG/BRG initiative change effort might begin with enthusiasm and excitement but will quickly fizzle out.

Applying a Framework for Implementing Strategic Initiatives

Given that the diversity and inclusion process and the framework that drives its results involve change (both personal and organizational change), it is critical that ERG/BRG initiatives include a culture change strategy and process.

Our **Hubbard ERG/BRG initiatives Implementation and Transformation Stages Model** supports and is aligned with a business performance improvement framework. Therefore it involves assisting an organization through the following stages:

- **Stage 1: Awareness and Start-up** - This stage lays the foundational awareness needed to transition and apply the ERG/BRG initiatives in a diversity and inclusion oriented culture. It also provides the rationale and business case for making the transition.
- **Stage 2: Foundation and Strategy Building** – This stage implements the ERG/BRG initiatives visioning

and strategy formulation process. It helps to firmly root the ERG/BRG initiatives into proven approaches that successfully drive business related outcomes.

- **Stage 3: Integrating Culture and Systems** – This stage generates the culture and systems infrastructure building process which is aligned with and in support of the organization's business strategy. It helps to infuse the ERG/BRG initiatives into the way the organization naturally does business and is in alignment with business objectives at all levels.
- **Stage 4: Building Strategic Capability** – This stage supports and guides individuals in building personal and other competencies to develop skills to solve team and organization problems (building strategic solutions) using ERG/BRG initiatives as the basis of those efforts.
- **Stage 5: Innovation and Breakthrough Performance** – This stage integrates ERG/BRG initiatives and diverse workforce innovation which utilizes creativity in appropriate areas of the organization to produce measurable results and generate a financial and non-financial ROI.

These five stages help set expectations of the ERG/BRG initiative change process and lay the groundwork for its continued evolution and development. It also identifies the transition stages to take ERG/BRG initiatives and the organization to "the next level" of capability and performance using ERG/BRG approaches as strategic solutions to organizational challenges.

Hubbard Diversity Transition and Transformation Stages Model

Stage 1	Stage 2	Stage 3	Stage 4	Stage 5
Awareness and Start-up	*Foundation and Strategy Building*	*Integrating Culture and Systems*	*Building strategic Capability*	*Innovation and Break-through Performance*

To produce this outcome, most interventions will require a formal change management methodology (with identifiable stages) that creates a roadmap for an organization's change and transformation. We have found the discussion and application of this model to be helpful, insightful, and instructive to produce the successful implementation of ERG/BRG initiatives.

Permanent White Water

Today, organizational change is so constant that Peter Vaill created the metaphor *"Permanent White Water"* to describe the state of change in organizational life. If you have ever gone white-water rafting, you know what it takes to handle the white-water environment competently. First, no one does it alone; you are always part of a team. Secondly, the team always has a leader, although leadership can shift. The leader's job is to keep his or her eye on the course, to look for obstacles, and to think strategically before giving directions. Cooperation is necessary in white water. Balance is critical. These same skills are essential in the white-water environment of diversity measurement and management. Fierce competition has forced organizations to rethink previously sacred approaches and to accept rapid, geometrically complex change as part and parcel of the everyday organizing process that is, ultimately, essential to survival (Hubbard, 1994). If ERG/BRG initiatives are to be successful, they must be built to navigate organizational "white waters".

Today, we face an increasingly pressing challenge to success: the need to manage organizational change and to improve organizational and product quality. In recent years, a great deal of literature has been written focusing on the need to plan for a changing environment. In fact, some organizations have created entire organizational units whose mission is to examine the process and quality of change, and to plan effective responses for the future. The goal of these units is to create a systematic method for dealing with change through formalized procedures and processes that not only anticipate changes in the structure, technology, and personnel of the organization, but also implement them. Implementing ERG/BRG initiatives are critical among these tasks.

Change is a universal aspect of doing business. No business enterprise is exempt, regardless of its structure. Nevertheless, though change often presents a threat to survival, it also frequently offers unprecedented opportunity for growth, expansion, and learning. Today's managers and employees face the challenge of creating an organizational structure capable of remaining current, flexible, and viable to meet the needs of a diverse workforce and customer base, while at the same time remaining focused to contribute to the efficient and effective achievement of the organization's objectives. Meeting this challenge requires an approach that addresses both the structural and psychological dynamics of change as you implement your ERG/BRG initiatives.

Change as a Paradox

Organizational change is a process, not an event. Internal and external pressures exerted on the organization cause it. Paradoxically, a business's success depends on its ability to remain stable while managing a complex, evolving series of changes. Change without order and order without change can be equally crippling. To be effective, an organization must be anchored in the past, yet immediately responsive and adaptable to a paradigm-busting future where success is written at its edge. Thus, new generation employees are hired while older employees retire, move on, or come back again. Established products are discontinued while new diversity-friendly products are introduced. Old markets expire while new diverse customer markets emerge and are rapidly exploited.

The amount, direction, and speed of change may vary, but change over time is an inherent aspect of all businesses. Therefore, there is a clear need to understand change and know how to introduce the diversity change process in a manner consistent with a business's objectives and with the needs of its employees. What is known with certainty is that coping with and mastering change are acknowledged needs of the present and the future.

Analyzing Readiness for Change

In order to create an effective ERG/BRG initiative change process, it is essential to analyze the need for this change and the organization's readiness for the change. A simple formula for examining the dynamics of employee resistance and the organization's readiness for the ERG/BRG initiatives change process is as follows:

C = P(SV)D > R

Where...

C = Change
P = Practical First Steps
SV = Shared Vision for the ERG/BRG initiatives Future State
D = Dissatisfaction with Current State
R = Resistance

Translated, this formula suggests that in order to manage an ERG/BRG initiative change effort successfully, a concrete plan to get to the ERG/BRG initiative change state, a clear, shared vision of the ERG/BRG initiatives future state after implementation, and the level of dissatisfaction in the system with the current organizational state (such as poorly designed products for emerging diverse customer markets that have resulted in decreased revenues, etc.) must combine to be greater than employee resistance to change in order for the ERG/BRG initiative change effort to have a chance at success. It suggests that a shared ERG/BRG initiatives vision and practical first steps are key elements to build along with selling the need to change (a component of which includes developing a measurement-based ERG/BRG initiative business case).

We must keep in mind that employee resistance to change is natural and common. It is unrealistic to think otherwise. In fact, some resistance is healthy for the organization. It allows the organization to challenge itself regarding the need for change by answering employee questions and building data-based responses. Employee resistance prompts the organization to take a good hard look at the circumstances that make the change necessary and puts pressure on the agents of change to clearly inform employees and builds commitment. Instead of balking at resistance, the ERG/BRG initiative change agent should anticipate it and see it as a normal reaction to organizational change and not necessarily an affront on the ERG/BRG initiative effort per se (unfortunately, there will be some contingents in the organization who will be exceptions to this perspective) (Hubbard, 1994).

Many Change Efforts Miss the Mark

Most efforts at change fall short of their goals. As Peter Senge and his colleagues report, many of their efforts to create learning organizations did not accomplish the intended results! Ron Ashkenas writes that only 25 to 30 percent of change efforts actually succeed (Senge, Kleiner, Roberts, Ross, Rother, Smith, 1999; Ashkenas, 1994). James Champy shares similar findings about his work on reengineering, reporting success rates of about 25 to 33 percent. Clearly, interventions-no matter how well intentioned and carefully thought out-are far more difficult to put into action than we may think. Likewise, many companies believe ERG/BRG initiative measurement matters and genuinely want to create and use ERG/BRG initiatives. Often these companies express enormous initial interest in this approach, conduct a workshop or two about how to use ERG/BRG initiatives, begin to sort out which ERG/BRG initiative measures matter most, and track them once or twice. Soon, however, they discover that the commitment to the ERG/BRG initiatives measurement work was more rhetoric and hope than reality and action. In most cases, the technical aspects of ERG/BRG initiatives are manageable. With focus, executives can identify the right measures and create indices to assess them. But high-quality *thinking* about ERG/BRG initiatives as a change process never occurs. These companies fail to apply change management lessons to their implementation of ERG/BRG initiatives.

The trouble with implementing change comes not from misunderstanding *what* to do, but from a lack of discipline about *how* to do what needs doing. Becker, Huselid, and Ulrich found the following a set of seven keys and processes to make change happen that have convergent validity in that they are consistent with the research on other change models; they also have face validity-in that managers in organizations have confirmed that these factors help make change happen. Finally, the factors also have deployment validity. They have been used in their present or adapted form for thousands of change projects at hundreds of companies (Becker, Huselid, and Ulrich, 2001):

Below, you will find an example of the critical success factors that can help make an ERG/BRG initiative change process happen successfully:

Keys and Processes for Making Change Happen

Key Success Factors for Change	Questions for Assessing and Accomplishing Change
1. *Leading change* (who *is responsible*)	Do we have a leader... • who owns and champions the change? • who demonstrates public commitment to making it happen? • who will garner resources to sustain it? • who will invest personal time and attention to following it through?
2. *Creating a shared need* (why *do it*)	Do employees... • see the reason for the change? • understand why the change is important? • see how it will help them and/or the business in the short and long term?
3. *Shaping a vision* (what *will it look like when we are done*)	Do employees... • see the outcomes of the change in behavioral terms (that is, what they will do differently as a result of the change)? • get excited about these outcomes? • understand how the change will benefit customers and other

Keys and Processes for Making Change Happen

Key Success Factors for Change	Questions for Assessing and Accomplishing Change
	stakeholders?
4. *Mobilizing commitment* (who else needs to be involved)	Do the sponsors of the change… • recognize who else needs to be committed to the change for it to happen? • know how to build a coalition of support for the change? • have the ability to enlist the support of key individuals in the organization? • have the ability to build a responsibility matrix to make the change happen?
5. *Building enabling systems* (how will it be institutionalized)	Do the sponsors of the change... • understand how to sustain the change through modifying systems (e.g., staffing, training, appraisal, rewards, structure, operations, marketing, communication, etc.)? • recognize the technology investment required to implement the change? • have access to financial resources to sustain the change?

Keys and Processes for Making Change Happen	
Key Success Factors for Change	Questions for Assessing and Accomplishing Change
6. *Monitoring and demonstrating progress* (how *will it be measured*)	Do the sponsors of the change... • have a means of measuring the success of the change? • plan to benchmark progress on both the results of the change and the implementation process?
7. *Making it last* (how *will it be initiated and sustained*)	Do the sponsors of the change... • recognize the first steps needed to get started? • have a short- and long-term plan to keep attention focused on the change? • have a plan for adapting the change over time to shifting circumstances?

Adapted from Source: Becker, Brian E., Huselid, Mark A., and Ulrich, Dave. *The HR Scorecard: Linking People, Strategy, and Performance*. Boston: Harvard Business School Press, 2001.

The seven factors in the above table have been applied in multiple settings and thus offer some general lessons for successful implementation of ERG/BRG initiatives. First, the organization must attend to all seven factors in order for the ERG/BRG initiatives to succeed. The process of initiating and sustaining the ERG/BRG initiatives may be iterative, that is, you may need to cycle back through some of the earlier steps several times. But, in general, the process unfolds in the sequence shown in the table.

Second, you can use these factors to create a profile of your organization's present capacity for change on any given project, not just the ERG/BRG initiatives. You can generate this profile by scoring the extent to which each of the seven factors exists, using a range of 0 through 100, and plotting those scores as shown in the exhibit below.

Highlighting the quality of an ERG/BRG initiative implementation change process:

Quality of Our Change Process by Dimension

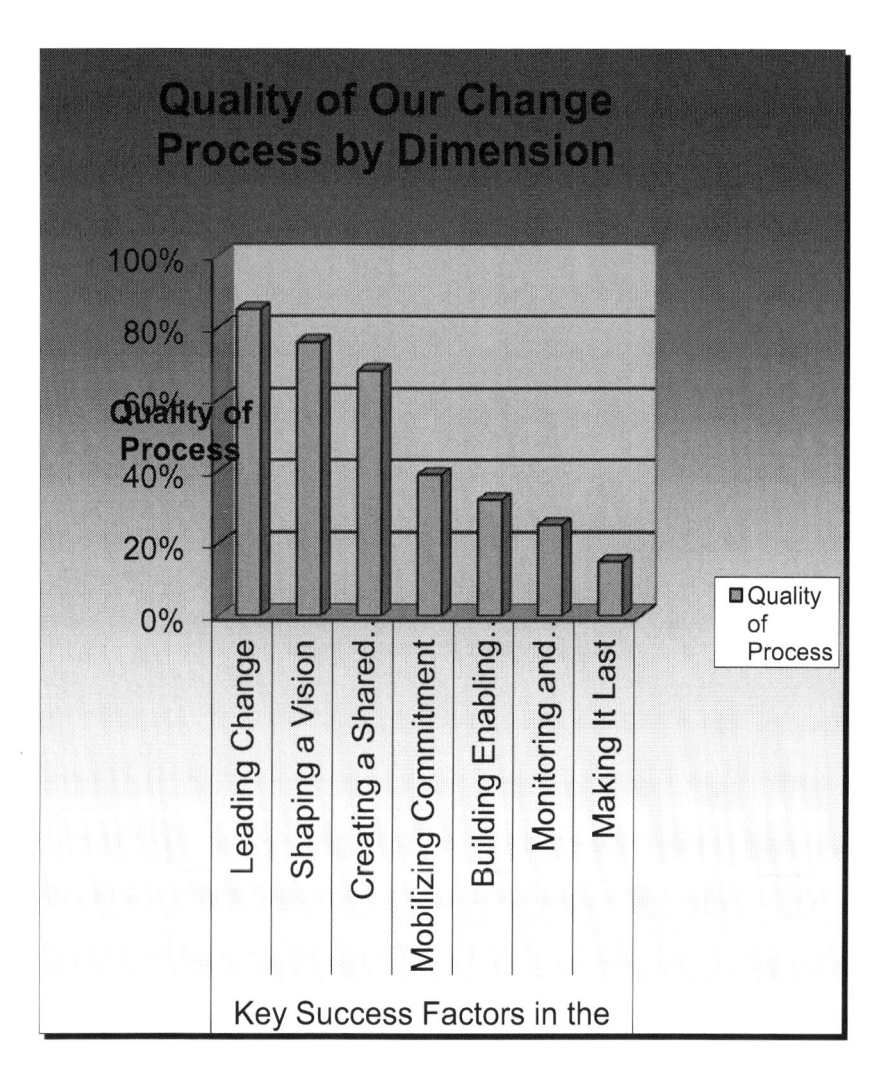

Y-axis: Quality of Process (0% – 100%)
X-axis (Key Success Factors in the): Leading Change, Shaping a Vision, Creating a Shared..., Mobilizing Commitment, Building Enabling..., Monitoring and..., Making It Last

Legend: Quality of Process

Adapted from Becker, Brian E., Huselid, Mark A., and Ulrich, Dave. *The HR Scorecard: Linking People, Strategy, and Performance.* Boston: Harvard Business School Press, 2001.

It is recommend that ERG/BRG initiative change leaders routinely assess the progress they are making on each of the dimensions of the change process using a simple profiling system such as the one illustrated above. During the planning phase, the profile could be used to inventory the strengths and weaknesses of your organization's *current* change process. When you consider past change efforts, where has the company been particularly effective and where have those efforts fallen short? This will give you a chance to concentrate on those areas where support and development is required.

The experience reflected in the exhibit above is probably typical of many organizations. For example, there is a reasonably enthusiastic cadre of change leaders, but they are only modestly successful at creating a shared sense of urgency around the need for change and communicating a coherent ERG/BRG initiative vision of the future if the change is successful. The change leaders understand the need for change and what the future might look like, but they haven't been effective at articulating their ERG/BRG initiative vision to the rest of the organization. Because the foundational elements are not as effective as they should be, the rest of the change process is undermined. It is very difficult to mobilize commitment to an ERG/BRG initiative change effort outside the core group because the message for the ERG/BRG initiative change has not been persuasive (i.e., a measurable business case with compelling evidence has not been presented). As a result, there is little support for changing other institutional levers, such as reward systems, that will reinforce and provide momentum for the ERG/BRG initiative change. Not surprisingly, there are no early successes to demonstrate progress, especially since no ERG/BRG initiative is in place, and ultimately the ERG/BRG initiative change effort never really takes hold and it becomes just another "flavor of the month." ERG/BRG initiative Change Sponsors should be prepared to answer the following questions:

Guidelines for Implementing an ERG/BRG Initiative	
Change Checklist Items	**Guiding Questions for Change Sponsors**
1. *Leading change* (who *is responsible*)	Who is in charge of the effort? Who sponsors? Who champions?
2. *Creating a shared need* (why *do it*)	Why develop these ERG/BRG Initiatives? How does it fit with our business?
3. *Shaping a vision* (what *will it look like when we are done*)	What is the desired outcome(s) of the ERG/BRG initiatives?
4. *Mobilizing commitment* (who else *needs to be involved*)	Who needs to support the project?

Guidelines for Implementing an ERG/BRG Initiative

Change Checklist Items	Guiding Questions for Change Sponsors
5. *Building enabling systems* (how *will it be institutionalized*)	How do we build systems to sustain the change?
6. *Monitoring and demonstrating progress* (how *will it be measured*)	What will we use to track the implementation process?
7. *Making it last* (how *will it be initiated and sustained*)	How will we sustain the effort?

As change becomes more complex, it requires holistic, systematic, process-oriented approaches. Many who are affected by the varied faces of the ERG/BRG initiative change process feel that it is the one element that keeps the organization in a constant state of flux since many people are still trying to grapple with the changes that are occurring on a global scale. This is not accurate. It's not the changes themselves that disrupt organizations it's the transitions to the new operational state.

Change is not the same as transition. Change is situational. It may involve a new selling location in another country, new boss of a gender different than the last, new diverse work team, new roles, or new policy such as consultative selling approaches in multicultural markets versus a simple product sell. "*Transition*", however, is the psychological process people go through to come to terms with the new situation. Change is external. Transition is internal. Unless an effective, systematic, psychological transition occurs, we can almost guarantee that the structural change to a new ERG/BRG initiative's processes will not work. Therefore, it is critical that we view the ERG/BRG initiatives implementation change in a holistic way.

What's the Difference?

According to the American Heritage Dictionary, the definition of the terms "change" and "transition" are as follows:

Change--1.a. To cause to be different; alter. b. To give or receive form or appearance to; transform. 2. To give and receive reciprocally; interchange. 3. To exchange for or replace by another, usually of the same kind or category. 4. To lay aside, abandon, or leave for another; switch. 5. To go from one phase to another.

Transition--1. The process of changing from one form, state, activity, or place to another. 2. The passage from one subject to another.

What becomes apparent immediately is that the definition of change implies an instant substitution of one thing for another. However, the definition of a "transition" suggests involvement in the journey, passage or process of moving from one state, form, place, or activity to another. This difference is critical to our understanding of the ERG/BRG initiative change process. The move to the new ERG/BRG initiative operating state may represent to others the complicated process of transitioning they will need to do to achieve the change state of an organization effectively utilizing the ERG/BRG initiatives.

It is essential to understand that it's not the "changes" that do you in it's the "transitions". If the "transition" is not effective, the "change" will not work. Transition is not a gradual or incomplete change. In change, focus is on the outcome the change will produce, that is, the end result. Transition is different. The starting point for transition is not the outcome, but the ending you must make to leave behind the old situation (such as becoming aware or sensing the personal impact of a changed workplaces after as the ERG/BRG initiatives shift the organization's routine). Using your own experience, think of any big change that may have occurred in your life: your marriage, your first managerial job, your first car, your first plane flight, or your first house. Perhaps each represented a good change, but as transitions, each began with an ending of the old way of doing things which took some personal and other adjustments.

In your new managerial job, for example, you may have had to let go of the old peer group you used to hang-out with. They were your peers no longer. Your new peer group may include people from races, and backgrounds you have not had exposure to. The kind of work you really liked may have come to an end. Perhaps you had to give up the feeling of competence that came from doing the work over a long period of time. As manager, you now were required to get things done through others. You may have had to come to terms with your habit of leaving work at the office, when you began to take some of it home or work late to finish it. These represent endings that began your psychological transition. Given today's organizational requirements and changing marketplace, great demands have been placed on organizations to deal with the need for rapid and sometimes radically different changes. Unfortunately, many organizations have dealt only with the need for change and have neglected an effective transition to accompany that change.

This can be seen when organizations announce on Friday that a major organizational (structural) change will take place on Monday of the following week. This is often done with no general employee discussion or involvement in the decision. Yet, on Monday, it is expected that the new organization will be up and running in its new form without a hitch. Unfortunately, in many cases it is felt that employees only need to be given a general reason for the change and they will comply.

This places a tremendous burden on the employees to "transition over the weekend," to come to grips with the flood of behavioral ramifications this change may and will suggest, such as acceptance in a new work group, competence to handle new responsibilities, perceived personal value for contributions made in the past being reflected in their new role, etc. For some, feelings that may have developed over a series of years must suddenly be reconciled because of the new mode of operation. Others may feel thrown for another loop and placed in turmoil because they still hadn't gotten over the last change the organization announced (which was implemented the same way). Thus ERGs/BRGs must take into account how they introduce their ERG/BRG initiatives to the organization that take the effects of change and transition into account.

Change handled without a psychological transition plan can cause havoc within an organization and destroy expected benefits. Change is often defined as setting something aside, abandoning or leaving something else for another. It can mean pulling a sudden "switch" on the employee without involvement as to process or transition. This can build immediate resistance to the ERG/BRG initiatives and could have been avoided to a large degree.

Building transition processes offer the best opportunity for long-lasting, effective change. Handling the psychological aspect of an impending change through transition allows endings to take place, adjustments to be made, and commitment toward the new beginning to be built. Effective transition depends on letting go of the old reality and the old identity (e.g., having a workplace environment or customer base that is not diverse). Transitions must start with effective endings.

To some people, change is a defense-provoking word; to others it represents a panacea. Oftentimes, change is presented as a zero-sum, all-or-nothing game that ceases to exist if employees don't immediately convert their behavior and make changes. None of these views, of course, is effective, since organizations and individuals require a reasoned, commitment-inducing approach for their involvement.

Effective communication about the ERG/BRG initiatives can make or break a transition strategy. The greatest benefit of good communications is obtained if it is done early, when the change to the ERG/BRG initiatives processes are being considered. Therefore, the most important communication planning is done prior to implementation. It is critical to pay attention not only to what (and how much) is communicated, but how communication is carried out as a process. Timeliness and credibility go hand-in-hand at this stage. The first step is to build commitment.

Building commitment to the ERGs/BRGs vision of the future through the use of the ERG/BRG initiatives must be a shared process from the beginning, not at the middle or end of the change process. A simple formula for accomplishing this is:

$$C = G(P)$$

Where...

C = Commitment
G = Goals
P = Possibilities

This formula suggests that the organization can build commitment by helping employees see a specific ERG/BRG initiative goal and asking them to generate possibilities for themselves or giving them reasons why the ERG/BRG initiative change will respond to the organization's and/or the customer's needs.

It is unproductive to institute an ERG/BRG initiative or any major change without foreseeing how many employees will experience this move for improvement as a loss of something they value. The result of this neglect is to waste valuable resources and to negatively impact internal and external customers at all levels. Every ERG/BRG initiative sponsor or agent responsible for the ERG/BRG initiative change process must be aware that either a hint or a full-blown announcement of the ERG/BRG initiatives immediately impacts an individual's value system internally. This impact must be handled thoughtfully and effectively.

Building a Rationale for Change

Change is more likely to happen when a clear reason for it exists. Moreover, the reason for the change has to carry more weight than any resistance to the change. The reason for a change may be related to danger ("we're in trouble if we don't change") or opportunity ("good things will happen if we do change"). Any change effort also offers both short- and long-term impact. It is important to share the reasons for change with those who will be affected.

Creating a shared need for ERG/BRG initiatives require understanding the importance of ERG/BRG initiative measures and how these metrics support the business's strategy implementation. Investing in ERG/BRG initiative measurement because other companies are doing it or because it is popular will not make the ERG/BRG initiatives sustainable. This book supports a unifying theme that ERG/BRG initiative measurement must be linked to business results. The ERG/BRG initiative champion should thus be able to articulate the potential outcomes of investment in the initiative. These outcomes might include better allocation of time and money spent on ERG/BRG initiatives, a higher probability of implementing the organization's overall strategy, more productive and committed employees, a more competitive organization, and increased shareholder value.

Sometimes, pointing to the need for ERGs/BRGs means asking, "How do we know if we've done a good job in implementing ERG/BRG initiatives "? Without measuring the ROI impact of ERG/BRG initiatives, this question often prompts vague answers based on the respondents' personal experience and assumptions about what "good" means. An effective set of measureable ERG/BRG initiatives give context and concreteness to these assumptions and personal perceptions, and anchors them in hard data. In clarifying the need to invest in ERG/BRG initiatives, champions should avoid some common pitfalls that will create resistance to it.

ERG/BRG initiative champions may also face potential resistance from ERG/BRG members themselves. As in any other function, some of these individuals don't want their performance measured. Being in an ERG/BRG without measurement can be a safe, non-threatening yet weak situation. With measurement comes accountability, and some of these employees may lack the confidence or competence to be accountable for the work they perform in their ERG/BRG. A ERG/BRG champion can overcome their resistance through extensive training and investment to ensure that they have the competencies to deliver against higher expectations.

For all these reasons, an ERG/BRG and their champions need to build a cogent business case for initiating and implementing the ERG/BRG initiatives. Skillfully crafted, this business rationale will inform line managers, help executives make smart choices, and guide and inspire employees throughout the organization.

Final Thoughts

ERG/BRG initiatives are not panaceas. They will not cure a poorly run organizations. However, they do provide a means by which you can collect rigorous, predictable, and regular data that will help direct your organization's attention to the most important elements of the change process. Constructed thoughtfully, ERG/BRG initiatives will help your organization deliver increased value to its employees, customers, and investors. By applying the seven steps suggested in this chapter, you can integrate the thinking behind the ERG/BRG initiatives into every key aspect of your organization's management.

While much of the work of ERG/BRG initiatives is technical, the delivery of the ERG/BRG initiative is personal. It requires that ERGs/BRGs desire to make a difference, *align* their work to business strategy, *apply* the science of applied diversity ROI measurement research to the art of building an ERG/BRG strategic management capability, and *commit* to learning from constant experimentation. When you create ERG/BRG initiatives using the approaches described in this book, you are actually linking ERG/BRG initiatives to the organization's strategic objectives for performance and results.

This book has laid out the theory and tools for crafting ERG/BRG initiatives with a Diversity ROI measurement focus. Clearly, no one can become a diversity ROI measurement expert after reading one book. Diversity ROI measurement is a professional, applied sciences discipline (like any other field) that requires intensive study, professional training, application and certification like that offered by the Hubbard Diversity ROI Institute and the Hubbard ERG and BRG ROI Institute. Nonetheless, by using the ideas and tools presented here, along with the assistance of a certified diversity ROI measurement professional, you can make informed choices about the proper diversity ROI metrics to use and help enhance you ERG's/BRG's effectiveness and credibility as a strategic business partner. A business partner that is clearly at the table, not on it for a budget cut or elimination!

References

Ashkenas, Ron, "Beyond the Fads: How Leaders Drive Change with Results", Human Resource Planning 17, no. 2, 1994, pp. 25-44

Bauer, I., Heinl, R & McGovern, C. (2003, June). Consultant Competency Model Role-based Analysis. Pittsburgh, PA. Development Dimensions International

Becker, Brian E., Huselid, Mark A., and Ulrich, Dave. *The HR Scorecard: Linking People, Strategy, and Performance.* Boston: Harvard Business School Press, 2001.

Bernthal, Paul R; Colteryahn, Karen; Davis, Patty, et.al., *Mapping the Future: ASTD 2004 Competency Study*; Virginia, ASTD Press, 2004.

Boyatzis, R. The Competent Manager: A Model for Effective Performance. New York: Wiley, 1982.

Brewster, C., Farndale, E., & van Ommeren, J. (2000, June). "HR Competencies and Professional Standards." World Federation of Personnel Management Associations.

Champy, James, Reengineering Management: The New Mandate for Leadership, Harper Business, New York, NY, 1995.

Hubbard, Edward E., "The Hidden Side of Resistance to Change", Global Insights Publishing, Petaluma, CA, 1994.

Hubbard, Edward E. *How to Calculate Diversity Return on Investment.* California: Global Insights Publishing, 1999.

Hubbard, Edward E. *The Diversity Scorecard.* Massachusetts: Butterworth-Heinemann, Elsevier Publishing, 2004.

Senge, P.M., Kleiner, A., Roberts, C., Ross, R., Rother, G., Smith, B., "The Dance of Change: The Challenges of Sustaining Momentum in Learning Organizations Currency Doubleday, New York, NY, 1999.

Sredl, Henry J.; Rothwell, William J., Professional Training Roles and Competencies Volume I, Massachusetts, HRD Press Inc., 1987.

About the Authors

Dr. Edward E. Hubbard Short Bio

Dr. Edward E. Hubbard is President and CEO of Hubbard & Hubbard, Inc., Petaluma, CA, an international organization and human performance-consulting corporation that specializes in techniques for applied business performance improvement, Diversity Return on Investment (DROI®) measurement and analytics, instructional design and strategic organizational development.

In April, 2012 Dr. Hubbard was an honoree at the Inaugural International Society of Diversity and Inclusion Professionals Legends of Diversity Ceremony in Rio Grande, Puerto Rico where he received the **Legends of Diversity Award** for establishing the "Diversity ROI Analytics" and "Diversity Measurement Fields/Disciplines"

The American Society for Training and Development (ASTD) inducted Dr. Ed Hubbard into the prestigious "ASTD New Guard for 2003". The July/August 2007 Issue of Profiles in Diversity Journal featured Dr. Hubbard as the "Diversity Pioneer" in Diversity Measurement. Dr. Hubbard serves on the Harvard Business Review, Diversity Executive Magazine and Strategic Diversity & Inclusion Management (SDIM) magazine Editorial Advisory Boards.

Dr. Hubbard served as Director, Developmental Education and Assistant Professor, African and Afro-American Politics and History, The Ohio State University. A sample of Dr. Hubbard's corporate experience includes Programming Analyst and Manager, Battelle Memorial Institute, Systems Analyst, Informatics Corporation, Systems Engineer, Xerox Corporation, Organization

Development and Education Specialist, Mead Corporation, Director of Training, Communication and Compensation for the 17 Billion Dollar McKesson Corporation.

Dr. Hubbard is an expert in Organizational Behavior, Organizational Analysis, Applied Performance Improvement and ROI Measurement Strategies, Strategic Planning, Diversity Measurement and Analytics, and Strategic Organizational Change Methodologies. He holds a Practitioner Certification and Master Practitioner Certification in Neurolinguistic Programming (NLP), a Neuro-science discipline. Dr. Hubbard earned Bachelors and Masters Degrees from Ohio State University and earned a Ph.D. with Honors in Business Administration.

1.5 Minute YouTube Introduction of Dr. Hubbard and His Diversity and Inclusion Return on Investment (DROI®) Measurement Work (From the International Society for Diversity and Inclusion Professionals (ISDIP):

http://www.youtube.com/watch?v=ZoVqbM9wty8

Myra K. Hubbard Short Bio

Myra Hubbard is Executive Vice President of Hubbard & Hubbard, Inc., an international organization and human performance consulting corporation that specializes in techniques for applied business performance improvement, workforce diversity measurement, instructional design and organizational development.

She has many years of successful experience providing consultation to executives, work groups, and organizations. Her consulting engagements support managers, teams and organizations to become more inclusive, improve performance and increase productivity.

She specializes in Organizational Behavior, Organizational Analysis, Employee and Business Resource Group Performance Improvement and Measurement Strategies, Diversity Measurement, and Organizational Change Methodologies. Her emphasis is on practical "how-to" approaches directly related to organizational goals and the empowerment of employees.

Her special talent and expertise in working with culturally diverse groups, enables her to readily gain trust, respect, and communicate well in many international, intercultural, and diverse settings. Her consulting work with organizations in the Netherlands, Pacific Rim, Korea, Japan, Samoa, and other countries has proven invaluable to the work she performs in the U.S.

As the President and co-founder of the Hubbard Diversity Measurement & Productivity (DM&P) Institute, she has a broad range of responsibilities such as diversity training, consulting, client relations, marketing, conducting organizational cultural audits and climate surveys, working with employee resource/business resource groups, organization improvement focus groups, executive interviews and coaching. She successfully applies her counseling, coaching background and experience to quickly establish rapport, and gain the trust critical when gathering confidential sensitive data from individuals and groups.

Myra is a member of the Society of Human Resource Management and the International Society for Diversity and

Inclusion Professionals. She holds a Bachelors degree in Business and Psychology, a Masters degree in Counseling, California College Teaching Credentials, a Practitioner Certification and Master Practitioner Certification in Neurolinguistic (NLP), a Neuro-science discipline and has completed doctorial studies in Business Administration.

Index

9-Step Method, 31
Accuracy and Credibility, 10, 156
affinity groups, 14, 18, 20
Aligning ERGs and BRGs, 5, 15, 27
alignment, 26, 27, 28, 29, 31, 32, 33, 34, 41, 48, 54, 79, 212, 213, 217
Alignment with Strategy, 7, 78
audience credibility, 191, 193
benefit/cost ratio, 74, 182
benefits of ERGs, 25
Business Assessment, 43
business issue
 business issue(s), 95
Business Needs Analysis, 6, 36, 53, 54
calculate ERG/BRG initiative ROI, 105
Calculating Diversity Return on Investment
 Workshop, 50, 141, 189
Calculating the Cost of Quality, 10, 148
Calculating the ERG/BRG Initiative Costs, 7, 11, 73, 181
Capturing costs, 166
Certified Diversity Advisor®, 39, 40
Certified Diversity Business Partner®, 39
Certified Diversity Intervention Specialist®, 39, 40
Certified Diversity Performance Consultant®, 39, 40
Certified Diversity Strategist®, 39
Certified Diversity Trainer®, 39

combined estimate
 Isolation Techniques, 127
Communicating Results, 7, 12, 52, 74, 201
Company Earning per Share, 33
confidence level
 Calculation, 116, 121
control group method, 117
Convert the Contribution to Money, 7, 9, 15, 73, 132
Converting Employee Time, 10, 149
Core versus Strategic Measures, 7, 80
corresponding benefits, 167
Cost Reduction, 46, 89
costs and benefits, 51, 165, 190, 199
Creating ROI, 7, 75
current measures, 97
Data Analysis, 7, 53, 71
Defining Return on Investment, 11, 177
Design and Development Costs, 11, 172
Developing New Measures, 8, 100
Diversity 9-S Framework, 59, 60, 61, 62, 63, 64, 65, 66, 67
Diversity 9-S measures, 67
Diversity Discipline Framework™, 41
diversity impact data, 119
Diversity Return on Investment, 49, 83, 165, 166, 179, 206, 242
Diversity ROI, 11, 37, 38, 41, 42, 45, 47, 48, 71, 87, 167, 181, 189, 208, 241

236

Diversity ROI study, 42
Diversity Strategic Plan, 28
Diversity Training intervention, 44
Diversity Value Chain, 8, 106, 107
diversity value-added measurement, 86
Dr. Edward E. Hubbard, 1, 209
drive key performance indicators, 24, 25, 26
DROI analysis, 176, 185, 186
DROI formula, 165, 186
DROI study, 176, 185, 186
DROI®, 6, 7, 12, 37, 50, 51, 56, 73, 77, 80, 83, 109, 110, 142, 144, 167, 181, 182, 183, 184, 189, 190, 196, 199, 200, 201, 205, 206, 207, 212, 213
ERG and BRG Deliverables, 7, 76
ERG and BRG measurement study, 55
ERG or BRG measurement system, 75
ERG/BRG initiative change effort, 216, 222, 230
ERG/BRG initiative deliverables, 78, 80
ERG/BRG initiative measurement study, 54, 196, 197, 202
ERG/BRG Return on Investment (BRGROI®) Report, 55
ERG/BRG Return-on-investment " workshop, 86
Evaluation, 6, 11, 23, 45, 69, 72, 169, 175, 190, 195, 196, 197, 198, 199, 200, 201
four Phases, 28
General Reporting Principles, 11, 190

hard data, 56, 133, 134, 135, 152, 154, 157, 160, 162, 184, 239
Historical Data, 8, 97
Hubbard Diversity 9-S Framework, 57
Hubbard Diversity Measurement and Productivity (HDM&P) Institute, 38
Hubbard ERG and BRG ROI Institute, 48, 85, 241
Hubbard ERG/BRG ROI Analysis Model, 101
Hubbard ERG/BRG ROI Analysis Model^{tm}, 1, 51, 52, 53, 72
human capital plan, 61
Implementation Plan, 12, 16, 215
implementation strategy, 30
increased market penetration, 35
Institutionalizing ERG/BRG Measurement, 12, 214
Intangible Benefits, 7, 11, 74, 184
Integrated Picture, 7, 67
interest groups, 14, 18
Internal and External Experts' Input, 10, 152
Isolate, 8, 15, 103
Isolating Diversity's Contribution, 7, 52, 72
Key Performance Indicators, 55
key questions
  For Reporting ROI, 51, 194
Making Change Happen, 225
Management Estimate Isolation Techniques, 9, 128
measurement strategy, 34, 82
Measuring Diversity Results
MDR Workshop, 101

MetricLINK®
  Online DROI Services, 12, 208
multicultural marketing program, 116
National Black Employees Caucus, 20
Needs Analysis, 43, 44, 45, 54, 111
Needs Assessment, 11, 169, 171
Net Income, 33
Net Profit as a Percent of Sales, 33
Participant Estimates, 9, 113
Permanent White Water, 219
Prepare and Collect Data, 8, 15, 85
Product innovation, 77
psychological transition plan, 236
Readiness for Change, 12, 221
Reporting & Tracking Progress, 7, 74
Revenue growth, 76
Revenue per Customer, 46
ROI numbers, 33
ROI value, 16, 42, 87
ROI-based competency model, 71
ROI-based metrics, 32
Selecting the Appropriate Strategy, 10, 154
Share of Market, 46
soft data, 15, 56, 135, 136, 137, 138, 140, 144, 152, 153, 154, 160, 162, 184, 200
Strategic Alignment, 87, 208
strategic business partners, 36, 47
Strategic efficiency measures, 82

strategies available to convert data, 141, 142
strategies to convert, 15, 137
Supervisor Estimates, 9, 123, 124
The Hubbard ERG BRG ROI Analysis Model, 6, 15, 50
Top management, 29, 34, 59
Tracking and Assessing Progress, 7, 12, 16, 52, 75, 205
Transformation Stages Model for implementation, 216
Typical Cost Categories, 10, 168
Using Historical Costs, 10, 151
Value-added Results, 8, 87, 89, 90, 93
Workforce Profile Perspective, 41
Workplace Climate and Culture Profile Perspective, 42
Xerox Corporation, 20

Hubbard & Hubbard, Inc. Products and Services

http://www.ergandbrgroiinstitute.com/

Join Us! We can help increase your Group's effectiveness and bottom line impact. As a member of the Hubbard ERG and BRG ROI Institute, you will acquire expert ROI (Return on Investment) services and ERG and BRG support resources. Our ERG and BRG Institute team of experts will provide critical advice, tools, templates and processes that produce a value-added ROI impact for all of your initiatives.

Let us help you create an entire ERG and BRG strategy and ERG and BRG process from concept to delivery, as we have for many Fortune 500™ and Fortune 100™ companies around the world.

We can help you measure the Return on Investment (ROI) impact of any Employee Resource Group's (ERGs) and Business Resource Group's (BRGs) initiative as well as any other initiatives, goals and strategies.

As a member, you will have access to ERG/BRG focused surveys, member development tools, automated ROI calculators, worksheets, templates, case studies, over 300 formulas, and much, much, more!

Metriclink Dashboard and Scorecard Services

MetricLINK®

Comprehensive Online Performance Measurement and Management Services for Organizational Excellence

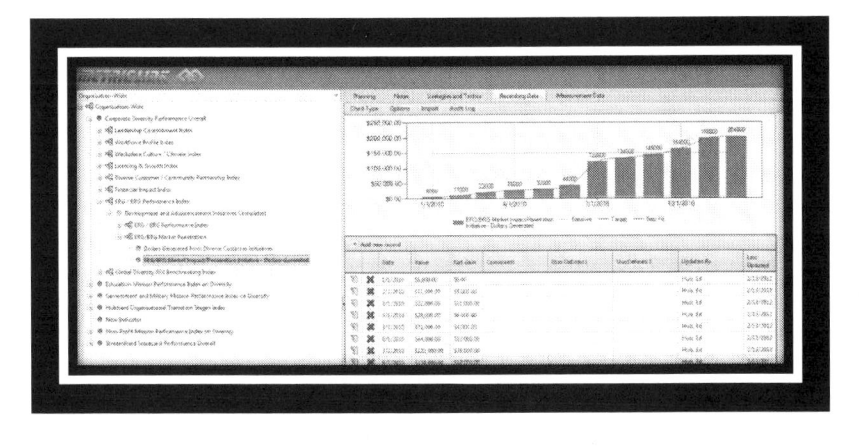

Now you can develop, track, analyze and report your ERG and BRG ROI initiatives using a state-of-the-art online service that was designed with ERGs and BRGs in mind. Practical and easy-to-use, this service gives your group an advanced project planning and Diversity ROI analytics tool to demonstrate your strategic bottom-line impact in data based, financial terms.

Performance Spotlights and Publishing Opportunities

As a member of the Hubbard ERG and BRG Institute, your ERG/BRG efforts can be showcased. Our Performance Spotlights (PS) is a place where Hubbard ERG and BRG Institute members can find ERG/BRG stories of success, learn how a challenge was addressed, or how an ERG/BRG was utilized for performance improvement.

It is a place where we spotlight and provide you with a strategy, tool, or tip. We can highlight the success of your efforts and enroll your Group's *ROI case study* and work in our **ROI Awards and Recognition Program and/or Publish Your Case Study in a Diversity ROI Casebook. If you would like to discuss a potential case study for publication, please contact us.**

Measuring ROI of ERG/BRG Initiatives and Other Webinars

We provide members with "tool-based" Webinars on a variety of subjects that are important to your group's growth and development. Check our site at http://www.ergandbrgroiinstitute.com/ under "Institute Events" for current details and programming. Our goal is to provide you and your group with resources and tools that help you drive measurable ROI-based performance that increases you success!

We can be reached by email message using the following link http://www.ergandbrgroiinstitute.net/Business-Resource-Group-Saint-George-UT.html or Call: **(855) 443-9147,** we are happy to help.